# Music For New Media

## Composing For Videogames,
### Web Sites, Presentations, and other Interactive Media

## by Paul Hoffert

Edited by Jonathan Feist

Interior photos by Brenda Hoffert and illustrations
by Paul Hoffert, except where otherwise noted.

**Berklee Press**

Vice President: David Kusek
Dean of Continuing Education: Debbie Cavalier
Managing Editor: Jonathan Feist
Director of Business Affairs: Robert F. Green
Senior Designer: Robert Heath

ISBN-13: 978-0-87639-064-1
ISBN-10: 0-87639-064-5

**Berklee Press**
1140 Boylston Street
Boston, MA 02215-3693  USA
617-747-2146

Visit Berklee Press Online at
**berkleepress.com**

DISTRIBUTED BY

HAL•LEONARD®
CORPORATION
7777 W. BLUEMOUND RD. P.O. BOX 13819
MILWAUKEE, WISCONSIN 53213

Visit Hal Leonard Online at
**www.halleonard.com**

Dedicated to Quinton, my videogame guru,

who spent ten years guiding me through

experiential interactions with the new media.

# CONTENTS

## CHAPTER 3    Musical Identities    47

## CHAPTER 4    Functional Music    61

## PART III  PROFESSIONAL TIPS

### CHAPTER 10  Aesthetics — 175

### CHAPTER 11  Working Environment — 181

### CHAPTER 12  Finding Work — 189

### APPENDIX  Technical Info — 197

### WRAP-UP — 205

### ABOUT THE AUTHOR — 207

### INDEX — 208

# CD DIRECTORY

| Folder | Subfolder | Type | Filename | Author |
|--------|-----------|------|----------|--------|
| 02_Loops | Looped Tracks | | | |
| | | MUSIC | 01_Rhythm1.wav | Paul Hoffert |
| | | MUSIC | 02_Rhythm2.wav | Paul Hoffert |
| | | MUSIC | 03_Rhythm3.wav | Paul Hoffert |
| | | MUSIC | 04_Atmosphere1.wav | Paul Hoffert |
| | | MUSIC | 05_PumpingElectric.wav | Paul Hoffert |
| | | MUSIC | 06_ClubDanceBeat1.wav | Paul Hoffert |
| | | MUSIC | 07_ClubDanceBeat2.wav | Paul Hoffert |
| | | MUSIC | 08_ContemplativeSynth1.wav | Paul Hoffert |
| | | MUSIC | 09_ContemplativeSynth2.wav | Paul Hoffert |
| | | MUSIC | 10_AbstractAtmosphere.wav | Paul Hoffert |
| | | MUSIC | 11_EdgyGuitar.wav | Paul Hoffert |
| | | MUSIC | 12_ClubDanceBeat3.wav | Paul Hoffert |
| | | MUSIC | 13_CongaGroove.wav | Paul Hoffert |
| | | MUSIC | 14_ModernRockDrums.wav | Paul Hoffert |
| | | MUSIC | 15_12String.wav | Paul Hoffert |
| | | MUSIC | 16_CoolUprightBass.wav | Paul Hoffert |
| | | MUSIC | 17_LoungeVibes.wav | Paul Hoffert |
| | | MUSIC | 18_CrowdApplause.wav | Paul Hoffert |
| | | MUSIC | 19_MixedLoopSequence.wav | Paul Hoffert |
| | Transitions | | | |
| | | MUSIC | HarmonyTransition.wav | Paul Hoffert |
| | | MUSIC | KeyTransition.wav | Paul Hoffert |
| | | MUSIC | RhythmTransition.wav | Paul Hoffert |
| | | MUSIC | StyleTransition.wav | Paul Hoffert |
| | | MUSIC | TempoTransition.wav | Paul Hoffert |
| | | MUSIC | TextureTransition.wav | Paul Hoffert |
| | | EXCEL | TransitionCalculator.xls | Paul Hoffert |
| | | MUSIC | TransitionLoop.wav | Paul Hoffert |
| | | MUSIC | TransitionSequences.wav | Paul Hoffert |
| | | MUSIC | VolumeTransition.wav | Paul Hoffert |
| 03_Identities | | MUSIC | CityPulse.wav | David Hoffert & Paul Hoffert |
| | | MUSIC | CityPulseExcerpt.wav | David Hoffert & Paul Hoffert |
| | | VIDEO | ManyChoicesFewClicks.mp4 | Hoffert Communications |
| | | MUSIC | UrgencyTheme.wav | Paul Hoffert |
| | | MUSIC | XBadMonster.wav | Paul Hoffert |
| | | MUSIC | XHeroine.wav | Paul Hoffert |
| 04_Functions | | MUSIC | ActionMusic.wav | Paul Hoffert |
| | | VIDEO | ActionScene.mov | Film Ventures International |
| | | MUSIC | DramaticMusic.wav | Paul Hoffert |
| | | VIDEO | DramaticScene.mov | Quadrant Films |
| | | MUSIC | FunnyChase.wav | Paul Hoffert |
| | | MUSIC | HumorMusic.wav | Paul Hoffert |

| Folder | Subfolder | Type | Filename | Author |
|---|---|---|---|---|
| 04_Functions (continued) | | VIDEO | HumorScene.mov | Quadrant Films |
| | | MUSIC | SongOfFreedom.wav | Brenda Hoffert & Paul Hoffert |
| | | MUSIC | xylohumor.wav | Paul Hoffert |
| 05_Presentations | | PPT | PP_DCMS.ppt | Hoffert Communications |
| | | MUSIC | PresentMusic1.mp3 | Paul Hoffert |
| | | PPT | Presentation1.ppt | Hoffert Communications |
| | | MUSIC | SatieGymnopédiesl.mp3 | Hoffert Communications |
| 06_Web | | VIDEO | DetectiveOne.mov | NDi Media |
| | | VIDEO | GotHerbs.mov | Jonathan Feist |
| | | HTML | htmlMusic.htm | Paul Hoffert |
| | | MUSIC | PageMusic1.wav | Paul Hoffert |
| | | MUSIC | PageMusic2.mp3 | Paul Hoffert |
| | | MUSIC | PageMusic3.wav | Paul Hoffert |
| | | MUSIC | PageMusic4.mid | Paul Hoffert |
| | | VIDEO | PhotoShowAd.mov | Paul Hoffert |
| | | VIDEO | WeedsEugene.mov | Ian Cook |
| 07_Game | | VIDEO | Game.mov | |
| | GameMusic | | | |
| | | MUSIC | 1_attractor.wav | NDi Media |
| | | MUSIC | 2_startup.wav | NDi Media |
| | | MUSIC | 3_situation1.wav | NDi Media |
| | | MUSIC | 4_transition.wav | NDi Media |
| | GameSegments | | | |
| | | VIDEO | 1_attractor.mov | NDi Media |
| | | VIDEO | 2_startup.mov | NDi Media |
| | | VIDEO | 3_situation1.mov | NDi Media |
| | | VIDEO | 4_transition.mov | NDi Media |
| | | VIDEO | Game.mov | Activision |
| | SamplerMusicZones | | | |
| | | MUSIC | Music Zone 1.wav | Paul Hoffert |
| | | MUSIC | Music Zone 2.wav | Paul Hoffert |
| | | MUSIC | Music Zone 3.wav | Paul Hoffert |
| | | MUSIC | Music Zone 4.wav | Paul Hoffert |
| | | PNG | WumpaAttractor.png | NDi Media |
| | | VIDEO | WumpasWorld.mov | NDi Media |
| 09_Mobile | | MUSIC | 6PartMix.wav | Paul Hoffert |
| | | MIDI | 6PartMusic.mid | Paul Hoffert |

# INTRODUCTION

This book is about composing music for new media. It explains the unique requirements for composing interactive music soundtracks for games, Web sites, mobile media, and presentations. It details the complex technical jargon and idiosyncratic language used to communicate among creators of interactive content, and it has many practical exercises to hone your skills as a soundtrack composer.

After you finish the book and exercises, you will be able to compose and communicate your musical messages more effectively, particularly in interactive media. If you're serious about pursuing this field of music composition as a profession, you will have created a demo of your original compositions that you can use to help you get work. The demo can be your "calling card," when you apply for your first soundtrack jobs. In addition, there's information about how you can market your skills to help you find the right employers and to help them find you.

I've divided the book into twelve chapters, organized into three parts. Each part includes practical advice that will help you achieve a fluency and expertise in composing interactive soundtracks. The music and video tracks that are needed for the exercises are in the included CD.

Part I is about the basics for understanding and scoring interactive media. It describes what interactive media are, and why a composer needs to approach these differently from linear media. It explains sequences, loops, transitions between loops, acoustic instruments, synths, and samplers. It details musical identities, including themes, motifs, logos, earcons, and leitmotifs. And it spells out the many functions that a music score can provide, when married to visual content.

Part II focuses on the different categories of interactive media. It covers soundtracks for presentations, Web pages, videogames, and mobile media, such as cell phones and PDAs. It describes how the media types differ, and why they require different approaches to their soundtracks. The videogames section has a thorough discussion of game genres.

Part III has professional tips about making aesthetic judgments, working in creative teams, and business relationships.

There is an appendix with additional technical information.

Every composer is unique, and that's particularly true in the interactive field. Some of us bring a songwriting background, some bring classical or jazz fluency, and others come to the field with traditional media experience, such as composing film or television soundtracks. This book is for all of you.

Part **I**

# THE BASICS

CHAPTER **1**

# INTERACTIVE MEDIA

A listener's experience of music differs depending on the medium in which it is presented. Listening to the same piece of music is different if it is presented in a concert hall, as a film soundtrack, or on a CD. Composers must therefore consider the medium when they create, and for interactive media, such as presentations, the Internet, videogames, and mobile devices, many traditional practices and techniques must be replaced by newer ones.

## COMMUNICATING WITH MUSIC

Composers write music to communicate with an audience. A composer may communicate a mood or emotion with a symphonic work or tell a story using song lyrics. Whatever the form, music provides a universal language for human communication.

Music can be combined with other media, such as film, theater, the Internet, or videogames, to help define the characters, story, and setting. When married with these visual content types, music adds otherwise unattainable depth and emotion to the communication.

Music must be tailored to the medium in which it is used. The great twentieth-century media guru Marshall McLuhan wrote extensively about how communication is affected by the medium through which it takes place. His catchphrase, "The medium is the message," has become part of our vocabulary. It means that each medium of communication affects the messages it delivers in a fundamental way. A movie's message will be perceived differently in a cinema than on a small-screen DVD player.

## MEDIA, MESSAGES, AND CONTENT

A medium is an object or electronic system that carries messages. Examples include radio, television, film, videotape, the Internet, CDs, DVDs, newspapers, and books. "Medium" means middle or between; in this case, it's the device between the message's creator and the audience. An audience may consist of viewers, readers, listeners, or a combination of these, depending on whether the messages contain visuals, sound, or text. Members of an audience who take an active role in receiving the message are known as "users."

In this book, we'll focus on music in interactive media, such as the Internet, mobile phones, and videogames. In interactive media, the communication is two-way, sometimes called "symmetrical." Instead of passively experiencing a message in a theater or on the radio, interactive media users can send messages during the communication using a keyboard, mouse, controller, or other interactive device, thereby affecting the course of the communication.

Using interactive media is like having a conversation. When you have a conversation, what you say depends on what the other person has just said to you. Likewise, the other person's train of thought and words are affected by what you say. Consequently, interactive communication is not new at all; it is hard-wired into our DNA as an essential human function. This fundamental process, by which people exchange information and emotions, is more democratic and can be more satisfying than having a single speaker and an audience of passive listeners.

## LINEAR CONTENT AND MEDIA

The messages carried by media are commonly known as "content." Content may be informational, entertaining, functional, or a combination of these. The content in a story may be delivered by many different media: a television program, a movie, a song, a computer program, a game, an e-mail message, a Web page, a magazine story, or even a toy.

Some content is linear. Its message starts, continues uninterrupted, and then ends. For example, the nursery rhyme "Jack and Jill went up the hill to fetch a pail of water / Jack fell down and broke his crown, and Jill came tumbling after" is a sequential unveiling of a particular story content that needs to be told in a precise order. A young child who interrupts in the middle of the rhyme to say, "No! Jack and Jill went up the hill to play with the pussycat," will be told, "That's another story. In this story, they go up the hill to get water."

Linear content is well suited to linear media, such as books and television programs that have fixed lengths and are designed to be experienced from beginning to end. Linear media are well suited for mass communication (from a single source to a large audience) because everyone in the audience is meant to experience the same content. It's efficient to distribute such linear content by Industrial Age technologies such as printing or broadcasting.

Mass communication was the primary method of distributing linear content in the twentieth century. It's often referred to as a "few-to-many" system, because relatively few communications providers, such as record companies, movie studios, and television networks, send most of the available linear content to millions of people throughout the world. Each song, movie, or television program is designed to have an audience of many listeners or viewers.

You can determine where you are in a linear message/story by placing a linear measurement alongside it. Page numbers and paragraph numbers are linear measurements that work well in a legal document. Similarly, SMPTE time code, the time measurement standard of the Society of Motion Picture and Television Engineers, works well for media such as film and videotape, locating the exact hour, minute, second, and frame of any point in the user's content experience.

## INTERACTIVE CONTENT AND MEDIA

Interactive content requires users to take part in—to interact with—the content. Sometimes, a user changes the content by making selections, controlling how quickly events unfold, or by achieving a goal, such as reaching a new level in a videogame or filling in an online form.

An interactive version of the Jack and Jill nursery rhyme would allow the child to carve a different story path—her own story path. It might be, "Jack and Jill went up the hill to fetch a pail of water. On the hilltop, they saw a pussycat and played with her. When they came down the hill, Jack tripped on a stone and almost fell, but Jill grabbed him in time, and they got down safely."

If you were composing music for the traditional linear version of the nursery rhyme, your ending music would underline a tragedy. In the interactive version, your music choice would not be so straightforward. You would need to compose more than one ending because different children would interact with the story differently and each might have a different ending.

Following are some examples of interactive content that we'll be examining in this book:

### Presentations

A computer presentation using an application like Microsoft's PowerPoint allows a presenter to interact with content that has been organized into slides—screens of content that may contain text, audio, video, and still images. By pressing computer keys or remote-control buttons, the presenter can advance the show, one slide at a time. The audience experiences the combined content of the slides and the presenter's narrative. The presenter can control the length of each slide and the pace of dynamic content within each slide. For example, the presenter can make text appear on cue.

## Games

Games are available on computers, home gaming consoles, portable gaming consoles, interactive television (iTV), and in public arcades. The game code can be built into a unit's ROM, on a CD, a DVD, a game cartridge, a ROM card, or downloaded from the Internet. Once a game is running, the player continually interacts with it, sending signals to the game engine via hand and sometimes foot or voice controllers. Interactive controllers allow players to select options and to control onscreen characters and events in real time.

Interactive media are systems and devices that deliver interactive content. Unlike linear media, they are designed to allow users to interact with content. Following are a few examples of interactive media:

## The World Wide Web

Web technology is based on named pages (screens) filled with content whose placement and interactive potential are described by HTML—Hypertext Markup Language. Each Web page has a URL—a universal resource locator—that uniquely addresses the page and enables it to be located and accessed from anywhere on the Internet. In that way, a URL in an interactive document works like a page number in a book or a timecode in a video.

Each Web page contains HTML code that displays the buttons, pictures, or words on the screen and controls whether or not they trigger actions when the user moves the cursor over them or clicks on them. When a user's interaction with a screen element initiates an action, the element is called a hyperlink, or just a link.

By moving a cursor over or clicking on a link, a user can initiate a wide range of actions, such as jumping to a different spot on the same Web page, loading a different Web page onto the screen, or loading a music, video, or application file to the computer.

Computers in general and the Web in particular are interactive media because they're designed for users to interact with the content on them.

## Mobile Media

Mobile phones, personal information managers (PIMs), pocket PCs, MP3 players, and portable audio and video players are all part of the new and growing category of interactive media. Because they are small, lightweight, and not connected to the electricity grid, mobile media present challenges for user interactions, such as tiny buttons, small screens, and limited battery life. Nonetheless, their enormous popularity and the trend to merge many different functions into single devices are testament to the appeal of portable devices that we can take to school, work, or play.

Mobile media are interactive because they are designed for users to interact with the content on them by pressing buttons and keys, using styli, speaking into microphones, and so on.

## COMPOSING INTERACTIVE SOUNDTRACKS

Interactive media let users determine their story flows, and so interactive soundtracks must be composed accordingly, providing musical options that match the story options. Videogame designers often speak of each player experiencing a unique movie, and that means each user must also experience a unique music soundtrack. Clearly, composing interactive music is much different than composing traditional linear music.

Even if you can write a great song, compose a great symphony, or even score a great film soundtrack, you might not know how to write music effectively for a Web site or a cellphone game. Some soundtrack composers assume that writing for interactive media is basically the same as what they've done before—marrying music with changing visual images. While some aspects of interactive composing are the same, the fundamental issue of how you use music to tell the story is completely different. That's why uninformed film and television composers often experience a rude awakening when they first try their hands at interactive music.

Interactive media composers usually work as part of creative teams consisting of production managers, writers, navigation designers, graphic designers, interactivity designers, and software coders. In interactive media, the control of the musical forms and emotional curves must be shared with these team members, and also, perhaps most importantly, with users whose key-presses and other interactions cause the storyline to branch and progress in unpredictable directions. Some composers find the interactive environment liberating and invigorating, while others find it suffocating.

Composing music used to require the creation of a paper music score, with music notation handwritten on page sheets. That led to the use of the term "scoring" to refer to the act of composing or orchestrating music, as in scoring a musical or scoring a film. When composers began using computers to process their music creations, they continued to use the term "score," even when the music was played on a digital keyboard and captured by a computer program. The terms "score" and "scoring" are used for interactive media as well, referring to the sum of the music cues and the act of creating them. The term "music soundtrack" is used more or less interchangeably with music score, but has other meanings as well, including the record album from a film or game.

## LINEAR VERSUS INTERACTIVE CONTENT

Below is a flow chart of a traditional narrative story line. The writer creates the setting, characters, and conflict, and then adds plot points that ultimately build to a climax. Finally, the conflict is resolved and the story ends.

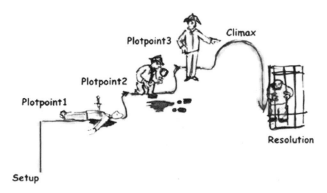

**Fig. 1.1.** Linear Story. Illustration by Eli Kassner.

Linear narratives on film, video, or audio media have fixed running times—the time from start to finish. The message path (story) is the same for every user, every time. That's not the case with interactive content, which has many points in the story path that allow for branching. Branching of a story is much like its namesake on a tree. You go along the main trunk until it splits into several branches. Then you must decide which one to take. Some branches are longer than others. Some branches end if you follow them, while others give rise to more branches, and so on.

The following interactive story diagram illustrates the point. In this diagram, there are twenty-four scenes that relate to each other in a manner that looks more like a bush than a tree. For someone inexperienced in reading interactive scripts, it's pretty confusing. We'll come back to this illustration and help make more sense of it later in this chapter, after explaining how interactive flow works.

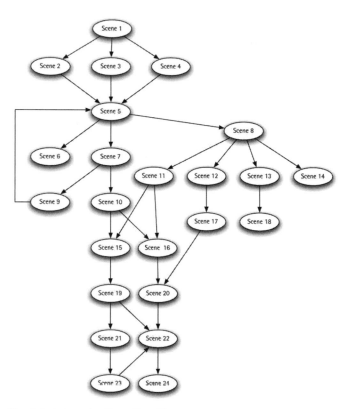

**Fig. 1.2.** Interactive Story Flow Chart

# RUNNING TIME VERSUS TOTAL SCENE TIME

The running time for an interactive story depends on which story paths (branches) a user chooses. The interactive composer must create music for all story branches (scenes), while the user may experience only a small fraction of these in a much shorter running time. An interactive story that unfolds to a user in ten minutes might require an hour or more of scenes and associated music cues. On the other hand, if many scenes are repeated (think of a videogame in which you might play certain levels twenty or thirty times before moving on), the running time could be much longer than the cumulative time of the individual scenes.

Here's a practical example of why this matters to composers of interactive soundtracks. Let's say a composer gets a call to bid on the music soundtrack for an interactive marketing DVD that will be installed in a kiosk in a mall. Each passer-by that activates the screen will watch a somewhat customized story, depending on which choices are made at certain points in the message. The composer asks how long the message video will be and is told that it will run about five minutes, divided into three sections—an opening, middle, and ending.

If this were a linear video, the composer would quote a price on composing five minutes of music divided into three cues. However, for an interactive production, the composer would not yet have enough information to determine how much music would be needed or how complex the transitions from cue to cue would be. Quoting a price at this point in the conversation could lead to a serious misquote with potentially negative financial results for the composer. The following two scenarios illustrate this point. Each scenario would be accurately described by the information provided by the production company in the example above, yet the workloads would be very different.

## Scenario A

The video message in scenario A has three parts, consisting of a fixed beginning, a choice of one of three middle sections, and a fixed ending. The selection of the middle section is triggered by user input about their age range, with one option for youth, another for adults, and a third for seniors. The opening and closing are each one minute long, and the middle sections are each two minutes long. The running time is always five minutes, but the amount of music needed would be eight minutes, made up of the one-minute opening, the one-minute closing, and three different two-minute middle sections. Different music would be needed for each middle section, linked to the musical tastes of the youth, adult, and senior demographic groups.

| | |
|---|---|
| Opening | 1:00 |
| Middle Youth | 2:00 |
| Middle Adult | 2:00 |
| Middle Senior | 2:00 |
| Ending | 1:00 |
| **Total** | **8:00** |

The total music needed would be five cues totaling eight minutes.

## Scenario B

The video message in scenario B also has three parts: a fixed beginning, a choice of one of ten middle sections, and a fixed ending. The selection of the middle section is triggered by user input about educational background, marital status, and income, as well as age range. The opening and closing are each one minute long and the middle sections are each two minutes long, just as in scenario A. The running time is always five minutes, but in this case the amount of music needed would be twenty-two minutes, made up of the one-minute opening, the one-minute closing, and ten different two-minute middle sections.

| | |
|---|---|
| Opening | 1:00 |
| 10 middle sections @ 2:00 | 20:00 |
| Ending | 1:00 |
| **Total** | **22:00** |

The total music needed would be twelve cues totaling twenty-two minutes.

The workload for composing eight minutes of music for five cues (scenario A) is very different than it would be for composing twenty-two minutes of music for twelve cues (scenario B). And of course, these are just two arbitrary examples from the infinite number of possible workloads associated with a five-minute, three-part interactive kiosk presentation.

It's clear that planning for and composing interactive soundtracks involves a different process than composing soundtracks for films, television programs, or videos.

The example of scenarios A and B represents the simplest interactive flow, with only one conditional branch point and scene options of the same length. In most cases, the interactive flow among scenes will be more complicated and the scene options will be different lengths.

In a linear film or video with sequentially numbered scenes, you can be sure that scene 18 will always follow scene 17 and will be followed by scene 19. Not so with interactive media. The relationships among interactive scenes can be fixed, conditional, or repetitive. The following list details five common types of interactive scene progressions:

A. **Fixed (Linear)**. Scene x is always followed by scene y.

B. **Branching**. Scene x branches to one of many scenes (y1, y2...), according to a user selection or a random process.

C. **Conditional Branching**. Scene x branches to one of many scenes (y1, y2...), according to the state (setting) of program conditions when the branching occurs. For example, if a program character picks up a weapon, enters a room, collects a certain number of items, or fulfills any other predetermined condition, branching can be triggered, prevented, or otherwise influenced.

D. **Fixed Repeat**. Scene x is repeated a fixed number of times.

E. **Repeat Until**. Scene x is repeated until a certain condition is met.

Following is the flow chart from earlier in this chapter with text descriptors for the first few scenes, to help illustrate the relationship between an interactive flow chart and its interactive story.

| | |
|---|---|
| Scene 1. | A character is in a room, standing in front of a three-drawer chest. |
| Scenes 2, 3, 4. | User interaction determines whether the character opens drawer A, B, or C and pockets a gun, a rope, or a key from its associated drawer. |

| | |
|---|---|
| Scene 5. | The character walks into the dining room. |
| Scene 6. | If the character has pocketed the gun (drawer A), police enter the room, the character takes the gun out of his pocket, and then the police shoot and kill him. The character loses a life and the story begins anew. |
| Scene 7. | If the character has pocketed the rope (drawer B), he sees a window in the room, climbs out the window, and lowers himself to the ground with the rope. |
| Scene 8. | If he then walks to the left, he gets to the house entrance, goes in, and returns to the room with the chest. |
| Scene 9. | If he instead walks to the right, he gets to the street where he sees an ice cream truck. |
| Scene 10. | If the character has pocketed the key (drawer C), he walks into the hallway, sees a door, tries to open it, and finds that it's locked. |
| Scene 11. | If he takes the key from his pocket and puts it into the door lock, it opens. |

And so on....

Note that picking up a particular object in drawer A, B, or C sets a condition (state variable) that influences conditional scene branches later in the story. For example, the key is needed several scenes down the story path to open the locked hallway door. If the character picks up the gun or the rope, he won't be able to open the locked hallway door, and will have to return to the chest of drawers room until drawer C is opened and the key is pocketed.

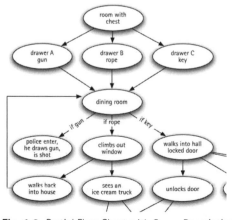

**Fig. 1.3.** Partial Flow Chart with Scene Descriptions

In figure 1.3, the composer would need to decide whether the same music would be appropriate for the character pocketing the gun, the rope, or the key, or whether different music would better underscore the different dramatic implications. Each of the music composition decisions would affect how the music cues would need to segue (transition) from one to another.

## HOW DOES INTERACTIVITY AFFECT MUSIC COMPOSITION?

The music associated with any scene or part of a scene is called a cue. Sometimes, in videogames, the production team refers to music cues as "songs," but you shouldn't confuse this use of the word "song" with the songs that you hear on the radio. We'll avoid confusion by sticking to the term "cue," which means the same thing in all media.

When you compose music for a scene in a game, you won't necessarily know how long the scene will last, which cue preceded it, or which music cue will follow it. These scene transitions may be under the control of the game player, who determines the interactive flow in real time as the game is being played. Still, the composer needs to consider how each music cue will relate to the music that precedes and follows it, no matter which cue it is, or at which bar or chord those cues will start and end.

This is different than composing music for a play or an industrial film. In those linear media, you know how long each piece of music will be, and you can create an appropriate beginning, middle, and end for it. For example, you may want to start a music cue very quietly under a scene so as not to bring too much attention to its entry, build toward a climax, then slowly fade out on a prolonged last note or chord. In an interactive production, the music will need to loop continuously until the user triggers the next interactive event. Using the traditional approach on a looping part would result in the music dropping out at regular loop intervals, inappropriately drawing attention to the music.

You may compose fifteen seconds of music for a Web site splash page, but the Web site programmers might want to stretch your fifteen seconds of music to fill the full duration of a user's time on the page, most likely by repeating the cue. Conversely, you may compose a five-minute cue for a Web page but a user might link out of the page after only ten seconds. In this case, you would need to join your music cue, now just a musical fragment, to the new music cue on the linked-to Web page.

When composing for interactive media, you'll also encounter unique technology issues. In linear media, you can synchronize music to an action such as a gunshot because you can calculate at which musical bar and beat the gunshot will occur based on the SMPTE timecode (see earlier in this chapter) of the event. In interactive media, the timing of a gunshot will likely be under the control of the user, so the composer cannot predict at which bar and beat it will occur. Music cues for interactive media must support this flexibility.

## EXERCISE 1.1. START A LOG

An excellent way to become a good interactive media composer is to make yourself aware of how music is used in commercial interactive products. Then you can draw on your experiences and learn from the best examples, while avoiding those that you think were duds.

Since the field is evolving and the lines separating content on one type of interactive media from another are blurred, it's worthwhile to immerse yourself in many media types, including CD-ROM and DVD-ROM, Web sites, mobile phones, presentations, and so on.

1. Choose a bound or loose-leaf book for doing the exercises in this book.
2. Start a log in which you record and analyze your interactive music experiences. Seek out examples from as many content types as you can, finding at least four examples in total. For example, if you're into action games, rent some simulation and RPG games, and note how music is used differently in each game genre.

## WHAT'S NEXT?

Now that we've discussed interactive media and interactive content, we'll move on to a discussion of the musical forms that are used in interactive content. Since a composer can't always know how long a music cue will last in an interactive soundtrack, it's best to use expandable music cues whose length can fill any time duration determined by the user's actions. The next chapter explores two musical forms that fit the bill: sequences and loops.

CHAPTER 2.

Verses, choruses, and movements are the musical

building blocks for songs and symphonic works.

Similarly, sequences and loops are the musical building

blocks for interactive music. These are the materials

from which interactive soundtracks are constructed.

## SEQUENCES

A music sequence is an ordered set of musical events. It's the principal formal structure for interactive music. We are already familiar with many types of music sequences in linear music, although they usually have different names. Sheet music is a sequence of music notes on a page. A music cue for a feature film is also a sequence of music notes.

The term "sequence" can describe musical materials ranging from a simple melody fragment (a motif) to a complete musical arrangement. A single sequence can contain melodic lines, harmonies, rhythms, string sections, and so on. Each of these musical components is a sequence on its own, and all of them taken together are also a sequence.

The sequence became an important content form when computers were harnessed for processing words and music. That's because digital devices process data one item at a time, in order. First, computers were used for word processing, which describes sequences (ordering) of letters and punctuation, so that computers can manipulate these into meaningful words, sentences, and paragraphs.

Later, computers were used for music processing, and the ideal representation was once again the sequence. In this case, instead of describing the order of letters and punctuation, musical sequences describe the order of musical events, such as notes, instrument descriptions, and sound recordings. Computers interpret these sequenced events and allow composers to manipulate them. Sequences allow computer programs, keyboard workstations, and MIDI recorders to manipulate notes, phrases, songs, and soundtrack cues in meaningful ways.

A melody can be stored in a sequence. The melody sequence can contain just its notes, or it can describe the melody more fully by including other musical events, such as vibratos, volume changes, tempos, time signatures, and even sound recordings—any musical information that can be represented digitally. More complex music, such as harmonies, rhythms, and orchestrations, can also be represented within a sequence as ordered musical events.

A music sequence can be thought of as a container for a chunk of music information strung together, just as a paragraph can be thought of as a container for a chunk of text information strung together. The chunk of music can be copied, erased, duplicated, or manipulated (sped up, slowed down, pitch-shifted, quantized, and so on).

The music sequence's versatility has made it the basic building block for interactive media music, since interactive media are digital and require musical forms that enable the synchronization of music cues with onscreen and interactive events. Today, all music for interactive media is mocked up, demo'd, and ultimately performed using music processors that manipulate sequences.

## SEQUENCERS

Not surprisingly, music processors are called sequencers. Sequencers allow you to organize and reorganize sequences and interpret them as music. Sequencers come in two types of implementation: software sequencers, which run on computers, and hardware sequencers, which are self-contained. Most sequencers these days are software-based because users can update them inexpensively online and because the cost of computers needed to run them continues to decline. Hardware sequencers are usually combined with drum and percussion sounds as drum machines and with complete production tools (audio + MIDI + synths + keyboard) as music workstations.

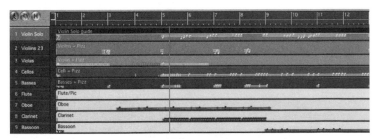

**Fig. 2.1.** Software Music Sequencer (Logic Audio Sequencer)

Software sequencers may be linked to a particular computer operating system (OS) such as Cakewalk for Windows OS, Logic and Digital Performer for Mac OS, or Rosegarden for Linux. Other sequencers, such as Cubase, Nuendo, Live, and Tracktion, are available on multiple platforms. Pro Tools, the popular digital recording and mixing system, is also a sequencer.

You can find free and shareware sequencers online at sites like http://www.freebyte.com/music. These sequencers are adequate for the exercises in this book, but are generally not up to professional standards.

Sequences can contain digital audio (sound) and/or MIDI information. Audio sequences contain sound recordings, like the files on a music CD or the MP3 files that are distributed on the Internet or on iPods. MIDI sequences, on the other hand, only contain information about how music is performed, such as which notes were played, the time intervals between each note, how fast (or hard) the note was played (usually on a keyboard or MIDI drum controller), and perhaps the patch number that was used on a particular piece of MIDI gear.

MIDI is an example of meta-music—information about music that can be used to produce real music. Since MIDI sequences don't have any sound stored in them, they need to be connected to instruments in order to produce musical sounds. MIDI instruments interpret the information in MIDI sequences and transform it into sounds that can be played through speakers or headphones, or saved as audio files.

## MIDI ACOUSTIC INSTRUMENTS

MIDI sequences can be connected to acoustic instruments, like the Yamaha Disklavier pianos. These instruments have mechanisms that play the piano keys in response to MIDI data from an internal or external sequencer. They work much like player pianos invented in the nineteenth century, whose meta-music is stored on piano rolls, an early form of digital sequences.

**Fig. 2.2.** Yamaha Disklavier MIDI Player

## MIDI SYNTHESIZERS

MIDI sequences are more commonly connected to instrument synthesizers—or synths—that take the MIDI data and connect it to one or more sounds in their digital memories. These sounds are usually organized into banks of sound generators that can produce many different instrument sounds at the same time. Synthesizers can produce sounds that mimic acoustic instruments or that sound unlike any real instruments.

**Fig. 2.3.** Rack-Mount Synth (Yamaha Motif)

Synths can be external to the sequencer, either mounted in a rack in the composer's studio or combined with a performance keyboard as a keyboard synth. They also can be resident in the sequencer (usually as a plug-in), in which case music can be produced from MIDI sequences without any external gear.

**Fig. 2.4.** Keyboard Synth (Roland Xa)

**Fig. 2.5.** Internal (Plug-in) Software Synth (Logic ES-E)

## MIDI SAMPLERS

MIDI sequences can also be connected to samplers—instruments that connect MIDI data to one or more samples in its bank of sounds. Samples are recordings of sounds, usually of musical instruments, that have been transformed into digital files. Sampled instrument sounds, when connected to music sequences, can closely approximate real acoustic instruments.

For example, you can make recordings of every note playable on a cello, each at different playing volumes. These recorded cello samples can then be organized within a sampler so that each MIDI note and MIDI velocity plays the appropriate cello sample at the appropriate volume. Voila! You have an imitation cello, playable from any MIDI keyboard.

Samplers allow you to manipulate samples in sophisticated ways, such as adding vibrato when a MIDI controller is moved, or layering different sampled instrument sounds together, so you can play a combination cello-plus-flute instrument, for example.

Like a synth, a sampler can be external to the sequencer (rackmounted or in a keyboard) or resident within the sequencer software, usually as a plug-in.

**Fig. 2.6.** Internal Software Sampler (Logic EXS24)

Most sequencers today can accommodate both audio and MIDI sequences at the same time, so it's possible to have a sequence that simultaneously plays recordings (audio files), synthesized instruments, sampled instruments, and even acoustic instruments (like the Disklavier) for a rich blend of diverse sounds.

## MUSIC FILE FORMATS

Fortunately, most interactive media industries use the same music and audio file formats—AIFF, WAV, or MP3 files, and these formats are supported by all popular sequencers. This means that composers need only master a single sequencer of their choice, combined with a few additional programs as their budgets permit, in order to create music for the whole range of interactive media including Web sites, presentations, CD-ROMs, games, and cellphones.

Chances are, if you're reading this book, you already know how to create sequences in a sequencer. If not, please refer to the many excellent texts and manuals, such as *Producing in the Home Studio* by David Franz (Berklee Press: 2004), or *Producing Music with Digital Performer* by Ben Newhouse (Berklee Press: 2004). Decide which sequencer is best for you by:

- making inquiries at music stores

- asking other composers at your level or higher for advice

- doing online research about specifications, features, and computer requirements

- reading reviews in music magazines such as *Electronic Musician*, *Keyboard*, and *Computer Music*

- browsing online musician bulletin boards, newsgroups, listservs, and chats

## SEQUENCES FOR INTERACTIVE MEDIA

Interactive soundtracks can be constructed from sequences containing audio recordings of musical ensembles such as orchestras, rock bands, ethnic instruments, and/or vocalists. These are frequently composed and recorded specifically for the soundtrack when the music budget is high enough to pay for the necessary musicians and recording studios.

Most console videogame scores are composed for and recorded with live bands or orchestras. Each audio music cue is then imported into the sequencer, assigned a sequence name, layered with synthetic music and/or sound effects, and treated the same as if it had been composed within the sequencer.

Hybrid approaches are common as well. For example, an original recording of a string quartet can be imported as a sequence track and then layered with MIDI tracks representing other instruments and sound effects. The sequence form is robust enough to accommodate any music that a composer can imagine for interactive media music.

Sequences can even contain algorithmic music, generated by rules set by the composer but influenced by interactive user events and random choices.

A sequence can be arranged to follow or be followed by any other sequence. This property lends itself to the interactive narrative flows discussed in chapter 1, for which the order of music cues is determined by the interactions of the user with the content. Sequences make it easy for composers to try out how different music cues will transition in different user scenarios.

The simplest arranging technique for sequences—one that has become the backbone of interactive compositions—is repetition. Almost all sequencers have the ability to repeat sequences. This manipulation is so common and fundamental that it has a special name: looping. A repeating sequence is called a loop.

# LOOPS

Loops are music sequences that have been composed and arranged so that their heads and tails attach seamlessly. They are designed to play repeatedly, so that no matter how many times you repeat a loop, it sounds as if it is being performed as a single musical sequence. That's why they're so useful in interactive media. You can play a loop indefinitely until an interactive event causes the music to move on.

When a loop is edited correctly, it produces a smooth, continuous pattern. If the editing is sloppy, you'll hear a pause, a hiccup, or a break in the groove. Loops are sometimes used as building blocks within larger arrangements and sometimes used on their own as the final music cue.

Looping technology has been available from the earliest days of music sequencing, but looping has become much more sophisticated and popular with the advent of hip-hop, rap, and dance music. These musical forms rely heavily on the repetition of musical loops that are combined from several separate tracks. Usually the process for composing this type of rhythm-based work begins with creating and/or choosing a number of compatible loops, laying them out on separate tracks, and then combining them into grooves.

## EXERCISE 2.1. MAKE A LOOPED SEQUENCE

The following exercise requires a sequencer that can play audio files. The required files are in folder **02_Loops** on the included CD.

1. Insert the included CD into your computer's CD drive.
2. If you have a sequencer program on your hard drive, open it. If not, find a free one on the Internet to try out, such as from the Web site http://www.freebyte.com/music.
3. Set your sequencer's tempo to 125 bpm and the meter to 4/4. There's nothing special about this tempo and meter except that they were used to create the sequences and will sound right on playback.
4. Copy the **LoopedTracks** subfolder in **02_Loops** folder on the enclosed CD to your hard drive.
5. In your sequencer, open all nineteen audio files in the **LoopedTracks** folder.
6. Set your sequencer to display the nineteen files on nineteen stereo audio tracks (one file per track) and set the screen zoom so you can see all the waveforms of the audio files. For now, mute the file on track 19 named **19_MixedLoop Sequence.** Your screen should look something like figure 2.7.

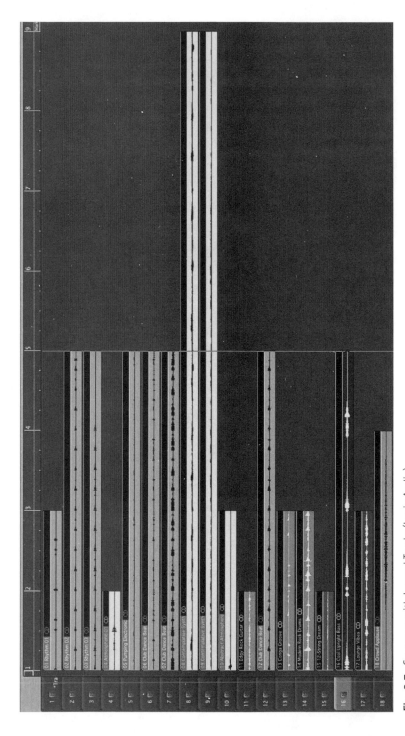

**Fig. 2.7.** Sequence with Looped Tracks (Logic Audio)

Each audio file has been prepared as a loop. In this exercise, we'll use these tracks to arrange a music cue for interactive media—a mixed audio sequence file that can be looped to score an appropriate presentation, Web site, CD-ROM, or videogame.

The following instructions will result in a sequence that should sound like the mixed cue named **19_MixedLoopSequence** on track 19.

**7.** Use your sequencer's tools to make either copies or aliases of each track so that each track file ends up in the following position:

| Loop Name | Source Duration | Assign to the Following Bars |
|---|---|---|
| 01_Rhythm1 | 2 bars | 1–16 |
| 02_Rhythm2 | 4 bars | 1–16 |
| 03_Rhythm3 | 4 bars | 1–4, 13–16 |
| 04_Atmosphere1 | 1 bar | 4, 7–8, 11–12, 16 |
| 05_PumpingElectric | 4 bars | 9–16 |
| 06_ClubDanceBeat1 | 4 bars | 9–16 |
| 07_ClubDanceBeat2 | 4 bars | 17–20 |
| 08_ContemplativeSynth1 | 8 bars | 1–8 |
| 09_ContemplativeSynth2 | 8 bars | 9–16 |
| 10_AbstractAtmosphere | 2 bars | 1–16 |
| 11_EdgyGuitar | 1 bar | 21–24 |
| 12_ClubDanceBeat3 | 4 bars | 21–24 |
| 13_CongaGroove | 2 bars | 17–18, 21–24 |
| 14_ModernRockDrums | 2 bars | 19–20, 23–24 |
| 15_12String | 1 bar | 9–16 |
| 16_CoolUprightBass | 4 bars | 5–16 |
| 17_LoungeVibes | 2 bars | 17–24 |
| 18_CrowdApplause | 3 bars | 22–24 |

**Fig. 2.8.** Loop Exercise Track and Sequence Assignment

Here's what your screen should look like. Note that different sequencer screens will look somewhat different.

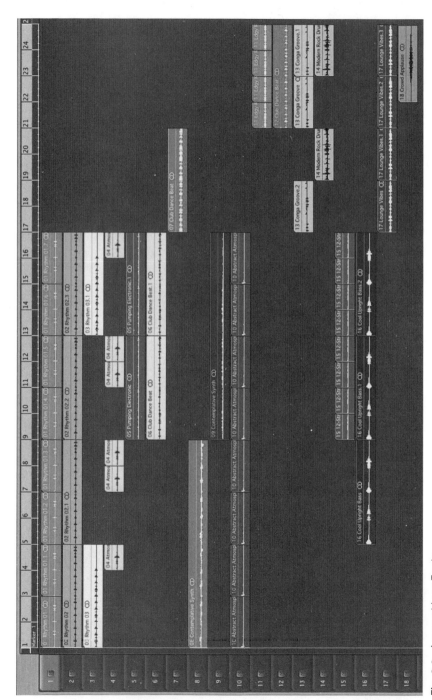

**Fig. 2.9.** Arranged Loop Tracks

8. Now, loop the entire sequence. This process will vary from sequencer to sequencer. Listen to how the transition sounds between the end of bar 24 and the beginning of bar 1.

Except for the applause track (track 18), all the other track sequences can be repeated (looped), with their ends fitting well with their starts.

9. Make your own cue now. Move the tracks around, delete some of the track copies, and/or add copies in different positions.
10. Use the volume, pan, and other controls to mix your cue to your taste.
11. Listen to your sequence and make special note of the transition from the end of the last bar to the beginning of the first bar.
12. Create a folder on a hard disk or removable disk named **DemoMusic**. Save all your music files from exercises in this book to this folder. When you're finished doing all the exercises, you'll have the core of a demo that you can burn to a CD.
13. Name your mixed audio sequence **LoopMix**, and save it to your disk drive in the **DemoMusic** folder, in a subfolder named **Loops**.

## LOOP PROGRAMS

All the loops provided in the exercise were carefully designed to be an exact multiple of a bar at 125 bpm. This allows them to be layered and sound good together in a 125 bpm sequence. When you layer different loops that are not the exact same tempo, they don't sync perfectly, lose their groove, and drift apart over time.

Certain software programs are designed specifically for making loops. They solve the synchronization and groove problems by helping you set loop lengths to exact bar multiples, and then shift the internal timings of beats to correspond with the main groove.

They accomplish these feats by detecting transients (large instantaneous changes in volume) in the audio files that correspond to beats and sub-beats. The positions of these transients are converted into time markers. Each bar of audio is sliced into pieces (beats and sub-beats) between the time markers. These pieces are then reassembled within any specified tempo, at the same beats and sub-beats, though these will occur at different times for different tempos. The resulting groove retains the original "feel" of the rhythm, because the relative positions of the beats and sub-beats are the same as they were at the original tempo.

Loop programs are very useful for media composers, even though they are designed primarily for DJs and producers of dance, hip-hop, and rap music. The following looping programs each have their fans among composers: Acid, GarageBand, Apple Soundtrack Pro, Bitheadz, FruityLoops, Imageline, Live, Plasma, Phrazer, and Recycle.

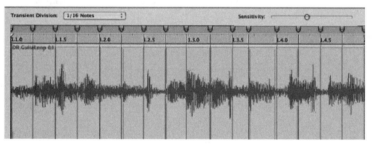

**Fig. 2.10.** Looping Program (Soundtrack Loops)

## LOOP TRANSITIONS

Loops are very convenient for interactive media because their musical chunks can play for an indefinite time period while being associated with a scene or scenario in an interactive work. By composing and naming sequences descriptively, it's easy to keep track of which music goes with which images. Programmers can freely repeat looped sequences, knowing that they will sound good at their repeat transitions.

It's important to try to avoid bumps in volume at the loop transitions (start and end of sequence). If a sequence starts at full volume and then ends with a fade out, it may sound acceptable when it segues from a previous sequence, but its transition at the repeat—the loop point—will sound harsh and emphasized. Alternatively, a sequence that begins and ends with similar rhythms can sound continuous, which is usually what a composer wants.

If a sequence starts and ends without any rhythmic components, the transition at the loop point can sound even smoother.

Many different fields have developed grammars for dealing with transitions. Language grammar uses punctuation to indicate how words should transition from one to another. Film and video have developed editing grammar, such as cuts and dissolves, to indicate how scenes should transition from one to another. And architects have developed grammar for making surface transitions at wall, ceiling, and door boundaries (moldings, frames, etc.). Pop, concert, and film/TV composers use music grammars, carefully choosing meters, keys, and tempos as well as music entry and exit volumes to achieve the desired transitions between musical segments.

Even more care is required for sequence transitions in interactive media. The transitions may be at loop points (repeats) or between one sequence and another that follows it. Musical boundaries expose changes in volume, tempo, rhythmic activity, tonality, harmony, texture, and style. In each case, the change has a psychological effect that can be jarring, smooth, or something in between. An effective interactive composer must be very good at managing those transitions to achieve the desired effects.

## Controlling Transitions

A good interactive composer knows how to control the transitions from the tail to head of each loop and between sequential cues. Determining how much contrast there is at the transition requires that you evaluate how different the music is at each side of the boundary. I find it useful to quantify such transition differences for each of seven musical elements that affect a user's perception. Taken together, these seven difference measurements make it relatively easy to predict the psychological outcome of moving from one point in the music score to another.

The seven key musical elements for transitions are:

1. Volume
2. Tempo
3. Rhythm
4. Key
5. Harmony
6. Texture
7. Style

Calculating these musical element transitions helps you control their impacts at the boundaries of sequences and loops— the smoothness or harshness at the boundary. By examining each musical element separately, it's easier to isolate the musical causes and effects. Aggregating the seven transition elements allows you to calculate an average smoothness or harshness boundary.

The point is not to end up with all smooth or all harsh transitions, but to help you control the psychological impact of your music. For example, Beethoven is well known for placing abrupt and dramatic key changes in his musical works. These transitions are disruptive of the music flow, attract a great deal of attention, and are frequently very harsh. Yet they are musically brilliant and provide the desired psychological effect. The following 5-bar excerpt from Beethoven's *Symphony No. 8* illustrates the point. In the second half of bar 3, the dynamics suddenly change from extremely soft (*ppp*) to very loud (*ff*). At the same instant, the key changes from F to D♭.

BEETHOVEN'S 8TH SYMPHONY

**Fig. 2.11.** Excerpt from Beethoven's *Symphony No. 8*

This type of transition is great in a symphony, but it would only be appropriate in an interactive music soundtrack if it occurs at a story transition point that requires a major shifting of mental gears.

Interactive music composers are frequently concerned with transitions that attract undue attention because they are not smooth enough. An important part of the composer's job in loop-based music is to deflect a user's attention from most loop boundaries, since these can become irritating and unduly emphasize parts of the narrative where the transitions occur.

Commercial loops are engineered so that their tempos, volumes, tonalities, and other elements have smooth transitions when used with loop-based sequencers. Consequently, the composer must overcome this built-in smoothness when the situation warrants it. Calculating transitions can be particularly helpful to composers whose experience has been primarily with urban music and loop-based sequencers, such as GarageBand. It's important that you know how to be dramatic and disruptive, as well as smooth and hypnotic. Sometimes you need to attract the user's attention when a change in mood is required, such as the approach of an evil menace.

The following approach can be used for transitions at repeats in a looped sequence, as well as for transitions between two different sequences whose playing order may be triggered by an interactive or narrative event. The calculator quantifies the transition changes of up to seven musical elements and arrives at a relative smoothness measurement that helps determine whether you will achieve your desired psychological effect. If the result is not what you're looking for, it will point you in a direction for changing your music so that you will be able to achieve your intended psychological goal.

For each element, the important decision a composer must make is how different it should be at the joint. If the sequence elements at either side of the boundary are very similar, the transition will be smooth. If they are very different, the transition will be more jarring.

Audio examples illustrating each of these boundary elements and a Transition Calculator file in Excel Spreadsheet format are included in the accompanying CD, in the folder named Transition Calculations. There is a smooth and harsh transition example for each element.

## 1. Volume Transition

A sudden transition from loud to soft sound or soft to loud is jarring compared to a transition between similar volumes at the transition boundary. Use the scale below to help you determine how different the volumes at the transition are. First, note the number that corresponds to the volume at the end of the loop or first sequence. Then, note the number that corresponds to the volume at the beginning of the loop or second sequence. Subtract the numbers, taking the lesser number from the greater in order to get the change indicator.

| Silent | | | Soft | Medium | | Loudest | |
|--------|--------|--------|--------|--------|--------|--------|--------|
| $ppp$ | $pp$ | $p$ | $mp$ | $mf$ | $f$ | $ff$ | $fff$ |

~~~~~~~~~~~~~~~~~~~~~~~~~~~~~~~~~~~~~~~~~~~~~~~~~~~~~~~~~~~~

| 1 | 2 | 3 | 4 | 5 | 6 | 7 | 8 | 9 | 10 |
|---|---|---|---|---|---|---|---|---|----|

If the tail of the sequence or loop is a fadeout to silence, the volume number would be 1. If the head of the loop or next sequence has a high volume, it might be 8. The subtraction, 8–1=7, indicates a big change in the volume at the transition boundary—one that will undoubtedly attract attention.

| tail (high) | 8 |
|-------------|---|
| minus head (silent) | 1 |
| **transition volume change** | 7 |

Note that the transition change would be the same if the tail volume was 1 and the head volume was 8 (reversed). Only the difference between the numbers counts, subtracting the smaller number from the larger one.

Listen to the **VolumeTransition.wav** file, in the **Transitions** subfolder of **02_Loops**, on the included CD.

2. Tempo Transition

Changing tempos—going from slow to fast or vice versa—is very noticeable. The following tempo line will help you find a number from 1 to 10 that describes the tempo at the head and tail of your sequence.

| | Slowest | | | | Moderate | | | | Fastest | |
|-----|--------|----|----|-----|-----|-----|-----|-----|-----|-----|
| bpm = | 60 | 80 | 90 | 100 | 108 | 115 | 120 | 130 | 140 | 150 |

~~~~~~~~~~~~~~~~~~~~~~~~~~~~~~~~~~~~~~~~~~~~~~~~~~~~~~~~~~~~

| 1 | 2 | 3 | 4 | 5 | 6 | 7 | 8 | 9 | 10 |
|---|---|---|---|---|---|---|---|---|----|

If the tempo at the tail is moderate, perhaps a value of 6, and the tempo at the beginning is also moderate but a bit slower, perhaps a value of 5, then the transition change would be 1—not very different and not very noticeable.

| | |
|---|---|
| tail (moderate) | 6 |
| minus head (a bit slower) | 5 |
| **transition tempo change** | **1** |

If you want to be more precise about quantifying the tempos, you can use the metronome numbers. The line for tempo has a metronome scale to help find the closest tempo match.

Using the example above, if the tempo at the end is 120 bpm (moderate) and the tempo at the beginning is 115 bpm (moderate but a bit slower), then the tempo numbers are 6 and 5, and a transition change of 1, the same answer as before.

| | |
|---|---|
| tail (120 bpm) | 7 |
| minus head (115 bpm) | 6 |
| **transition tempo change** | **1** |

Listen to the **TempoTransition.wav** file, in the **Transitions** subfolder of **02_Loops**, on the included CD.

3. Rhythm Transition

Rhythm is one of the easiest elements to quantify. Even casual listeners can tell when music is rhythmically active and when it's passive. Active rhythm will get your pulse racing and your feet tapping. Passive music is usually the result of a combination of synth or acoustic pads, such as slow-moving strings and an absence of rhythm instruments and rhythmic parts.

| Passive (Pad) | | Light Rhythm | | | Highly Active | | |
|---|---|---|---|---|---|---|---|

~~~~~~~~~~~~~~~~~~~~~~~~~~~~~~~~~~~~~~~~~~~~~~~~

| 1 | 2 | 3 | 4 | 5 | 6 | 7 | 8 | 9 | 10 |
|---|---|---|---|---|---|---|---|---|---|

Moving from a passive pad at the end of one sequence to a light rhythm at the start of the next sequence could be characterized as a change from 2 to 6 on the rhythmic scale. The difference (4) indicates a moderate transition change.

| | |
|---|---|
| start (light rhythm) | 6 |
| minus end (pad) | 2 |
| **transition activity change** | **4** |

Listen to the **RhythmTransition.wav** file, in the **Transitions** subfolder of **02_Loops**, on the included CD.

4. Key Transition

If you've studied music theory, you already know the relationships between keys. The following Key Wheel is a good tool for visualizing this. Joining sequences in musical keys that are close to each other on the key wheel creates a smooth transition. Those on opposite sides have a jarring effect.

NOTE: The key names are for major keys. Minor keys have three fewer sharps (or three more flats) than their major key equivalents. For example, C major has no flats or sharps, while C minor has three flats. E major has four sharps. E minor has one sharp.

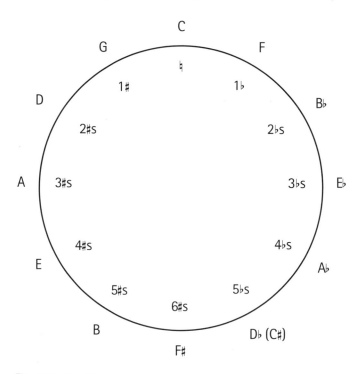

**Fig. 2.12.** Key Wheel

The simplest way to calculate the transition change for tonality is to count the shortest distance between the key at the tail of a sequence and the head of the next on the circumference of the Key Wheel, and then multiply by 2.

If the tail of a loop or sequence is in F major, for example, and the head of the next sequence is in A major, the shortest distance around the wheel is four keys. Multiply by 2 and you get a tonal transition of 8—quite high.

F major tail to A major head
**transition change** = 8 (4 steps counterclockwise × 2)

A transition from F minor (4 flats) to B♭ minor (5 flats), is only one step along the circumference of the Key Wheel; a very smooth transition.

F minor tail to B♭ minor head
**transition change** = 2 (1 step clockwise × 2)

A transition from D major (two sharps) to D minor (one flat) takes three clockwise steps along the wheel's circumference because D minor has the same number of flats as F major, its relative major.

D major tail to D minor head
**transition change** = 6 (3 steps clockwise × 2)

Listen to the **KeyTransition.wav** file, in the **Transitions** subfolder of **02_Loops**, on the included CD.

5. Harmony Transition
Musical intervals whose frequencies are based on simple frequency ratios are called perfect. These are unisons (1:1), fourths (4:3), fifths (3:2), and octaves (2:1). They sound very "locked in" when played together and are the basis for early music harmonies. They exhibit the greatest musical fusion or consonance. Over the past four hundred years, harmonies with more complex frequency ratios have become the norm in European and American music, particularly intervals of major and minor thirds (5:4, 6:5) and major and minor sixths (5:3, 8:5). These intervals, along with the perfects, form the basis for most popular music harmony. The remaining intervals of seconds and sevenths have the most complex ratios, and convey psychological tension or dissonance.

Another way to categorize harmony is whether it has a key center (tonal) or no key center (atonal). Tonal music was the norm up to the twentieth century, while atonal music is common in twentieth century concert (classical) music and some film scores. Atonal music is very likely to be made up of intervals that exhibit tension and dissonance. Twelve-tone music, introduced to concertgoers by composers such as Arnold Schoenberg and Alban Berg in the early twentieth century, is a type of atonal music.

| Tonal | Atonal |
|---|---|
| Fusion/Consonance | Tension/Dissonance |

~~~~~~~~~~~~~~~~~~~~~~~~~~~~~~~~~~~~~~~~~~~~~~~~~

| 1 | 2 | 3 | 4 | 5 | 6 | 7 | 8 | 9 | 10 |
|---|---|---|---|---|---|---|---|---|---|

If the tail of a sequence incorporates simple and consonant harmonies, such as those used in country music or Middle Ages plainsong, its harmony number would be low—perhaps 2 for the country music and 1 for the plainsong. If the head of the next sequence incorporates more dissonant harmonies, such as modern jazz or twelve-tone music, it would have a much higher harmony number, perhaps 8 or 10, respectively.

Moving from the country sequence to the jazz sequence would generate a harmony transition change of 6—8 for the jazz harmony minus 2 for the country (see A below). Moving from plainsong to twelve-tone music would have the greatest harmony transition change of 9: 10 for the twelve-tone harmony minus 1 for the plainsong (see B below).

A
| head (jazz) | 8 |
|---|---|
| minus tail (country) | 2 |
| **transition harmonic change** | **6** |

B
| head (twelve-tone) | 10 |
|---|---|
| minus tail (plainsong) | 1 |
| **transition harmonic change** | **9** |

Listen to the **HarmonyTransition.wav** file, in the **Transitions** subfolder of **02_Loops**, on the included CD.

## 6. Texture Transition

Texture is a measure of the complexity of music. Lots of different instruments, rhythms, and/or sound effects generate rich and complex textures, while just a few instruments generate sparse and simple textures. A full symphony orchestra playing with percussion would generate a texture of 10, as would a multi-layered pop song with rhythm section, horns, strings, synths, and vocals. A solo flute would generate a texture of 1 and a folksinger with a guitar might be a texture of 2.

Simple, Sparse                                            Complex, Rich

~~~~~~~~~~~~~~~~~~~~~~~~~~~~~~~~~~~~~~~~~~~~~~~

1      2      3      4      5      6      7      8      9      10

Moving from the tail of a folksinger sequence, a texture of 2, to the head of an orchestra in full bore with a texture of 10, would result in a transition texture change of 8—very high.

| | |
|---|---|
| head (full orchestra) | 10 |
| minus tail (folksinger) | 2 |
| **transition harmonic change** | **8** |

Listen to the **TextureTransition.wav** file, in the **Transitions** subfolder of **02_Loops**, on the included CD.

## 7. Style Transition

Musical style takes into account orchestration as well as cultural factors such as ethnic or national styles, as well as time era ('50s rock 'n' roll versus '70s heavy metal, for example). Popular music and soundtrack styles are very trendy, so it's important to understand that joining dissimilar styles at a transition can be jarring, even if the volume, tempo, rhythm, key, and texture are similar. Transitioning from one pop music style to another—from soft country to grunge rock, for example—can be more jarring than transitioning from soft country to a light classical style.

Smooth Style                                            Jarring Style

~~~~~~~~~~~~~~~~~~~~~~~~~~~~~~~~~~~~~~~~~~~~~~~

1      2      3      4      5      6      7      8      9      10

The style element has too many variables to easily quantify it, so for this case, you should let your ear and experience be your guide when determining the transition stylistic change.

Listen to the **StyleTransition.wav** file, in the **Transitions** subfolder of **02_Loops**, on the included CD.

## OVERALL TRANSITION CHANGE

The transition calculator requires that you input each of the music element change numbers for the tail and head of the sequences. It then calculates an overall transition change, ranging from 1 (totally smooth) to 10 (most jarring). You can get the same result by manual calculation. Simply add up all the individual transition element changes and divide by 7, the number of different elements.

The Excel file (TransitionCalculator.xls) lets you enter the change numbers into its cells. It will calculate the overall average transition change. In addition, it has a special key calculator that lets you enter the key letter and tonality—major or minor—for the tail and head. It then automatically calculates the key transition change. The one exception to the automated calculation is the style element, which you must estimate using the style line as a guide, inputting the transition change (difference).

A low transition change (1 to 3) means that a listener will hear the musical transition as part of a single continuous and flowing musical experience. A high transition change (8 to 10) means that a listener will be aware of each transition as a separate music cue with a clear beginning and end.

Here's what the spreadsheet looks like, using the examples in this section.

| Transition Change Calculator | | | |
|---|---|---|---|
| Element | tail | head | Transition |
| 1  Volume | 8 | 1 | 7 |
| 2  Tempo | 6 | 5 | 1 |
| 3  Rhythm | 2 | 6 | 4 |
| 4  *Key | | | 4 |
| 5  Harmony | 8 | 2 | 6 |
| 6  Texture | 10 | 2 | 8 |
| 7  Style | Estimate —> | | 5 |
| **Overall Transition Change** | | | **5.0** |

**\*Tonal Key Wheel Calculator**

**Key**
If key is minor, enter relative major

. . . . . . . . . . . . . . . . . .
| tail | head |
|---|---|
| C | Ab |

## EXERCISE 2.2. LOOP TRANSITIONS

1. Play the audio file **TransitionLoop.wav** on your computer. It's on the included CD in the **Transitions** subfolder of **02_Loops**. Set your QuickTime or Windows Media Player to play as a loop (repeat).

2. Input your assessments of the transitions of the seven musical elements into the Transition Calculator spreadsheet, when the loop repeats from its tail to its head.

3. Note the average smoothness at the loop repeat transition.

4. Now listen to the file **TransitionSequences.wav**, and input your assessments of the transitions of the seven musical elements into the Transition Calculator spreadsheet, when the first sequence moves to the second.

5. Note the average smoothness between the sequences. Compare their transition to that of the **TransitionLoop. wav** file.

## AVOID MONOTONY

There's a fine line between entertaining and boring/annoying, when it comes to music loops in interactive media. If you don't believe that media music loops can be tedious, just listen from another room while someone is playing a videogame. Chances are, without the compelling game play, the repetition will eventually get to you. It makes sense to avoid monotony in your sequence loops by making them more interesting, particularly if they will be repeated for long periods of time, while the user tries to arrive at the next interactive trigger.

Variation is a key to avoiding monotony. Hip-hop and dance remixers know this principle and use it all the time when composing with short repetitive loops. They usually lay down many separate tracks with looped elements in their sequencers, and then mute individual loops selectively in different parts of the song. The result is a song with sometimes subtle and sometimes blatant variations, creating the effect of dynamic change and emotional movement (cadence).

The process of adding variation to a loop-based composition is similar to that used by a live rhythm section laying down a groove. The musicians play all the bars in a phrase with the same general rhythm and feel, but they tend to make small changes in their patterns every two, four, or eight bars. The combination of these small changes builds interest and avoids monotony while keeping the groove intact.

## EXERCISE 2.3. MAKE A DRUM GROOVE

1. Make a loop of a drum part that's one bar long.
2. Copy the bar and paste it immediately following itself.
3. Select the 2-bar drum part and make it a loop.
4. Alter the bass drum slightly in the second bar.
5. Copy the 2-bar phrase and paste it immediately following itself.
6. Select the 4-bar drum part and make it a loop.
7. In the fourth bar, add a small fill to the drum part.
8. Save your file as **DrumGroove01.wav** in your **Demo-Music** folder's **Loops** subfolder.

The result is much more interesting and less monotonous than the repeated 1-bar phrase.

The same principle applies with larger chunks of music—looped music sequences, even when they are orchestral loops of twenty or more measures in length. You can use sequence parts like songwriters use verses, bridges, and choruses to build a song. You can add variety on a repeat by adding parts, subtracting parts, changing the key, or building longer structures by combining sequences.

### Variations in Loops and Sequence Repetition

Here's an example. Let's say you compose three 30-second sequences—A, B, and C—that are all in the same tempo and style. You can assemble these in the final project in any order you wish. If you specify playing the sequences in the order of A A B A A B C, for example, the user won't hear a repeat of the entire musical cue for three-and-a-half minutes.

Of course, you could just record the three-and-a-half minute cue as a whole, but delivering the A, B, and C sequences separately cuts the storage requirements to only one-and-a-half minutes of music. You can build a nearly infinite number of different cues from the sequences, including cues that randomly choose the component sequences.

## Variations in Orchestration

You also can add variations to your loop-based orchestrations. Here are some examples of change that require only a minor alteration:

- change the melody instrument(s)
- change the harmony instrument(s)
- mute the melody
- mute the harmony
- add or subtract rhythm elements
- add or subtract a countermelody

In some cases, the changed orchestration will require constructing a separate sequence (example: for a transposition). In other cases, if the playback device and software can layer multiple tracks in sync, you just need to provide the instruction to turn particular tracks on and off each time the loop is repeated. This is the most memory-efficient method.

Some additional compositional techniques that are quick to implement in a sequencer are:

- change the key
- change from major to minor or vice versa
- change the tempo
- change the instrument mix (track volume levels)

## WHAT'S NEXT?

Now that we've examined some important interactive music forms, it's time to pour some content (music) into them. The following chapter explains some of the most common uses of music in media: logos, identities, and themes.

CHAPTER

# 3

# MUSICAL IDENTITIES

The identity of a person, organization, product, or service is an extremely valuable asset. The emblem or statement that represents that identity is called a logo. Musical logos are used throughout radio and television media to identify stations and programs. They are just as important in interactive media, linked with text and image identities.

# MARRIAGE OF MUSIC AND VISUAL IMAGES

Music and visual images have probably been used together since the dawn of humankind. Primitive societies still practice cultural and religious rites that marry music with visual rites. Although no one knows why we have musical abilities, music appears to enhance and reinforce human communications, adding extra dimension and depth that can't be imparted otherwise.

Perhaps that's why music has been used to accompany film and television images from the earliest days of exhibition and broadcasting. The same has been true of music in interactive media, coupled with visual images on CD-ROMs, DVDs, the Web, presentations, videogames, and cellphones.

Something special happens when music is coupled with visuals. The mysterious neural connections in our brains that create our perceived reality store these stimuli as linked memories—a type of powerful relational database that automatically accesses an image when its associated music is remembered, and vice versa. These mental links between visual images and music are so strong that they have given rise to a shared vocabulary that's used to describe both music and visuals.

Words such as light, dark, bright, dull, blue, and colorful are taken from their original visual context and used to describe music. Likewise, rhythm, tempo, meter, harmony, consonance, dissonance, noisy, muted, cadence, and counterpoint are taken from musical contexts and used to describe visual images.

When music is synchronized with images, the two are usually experienced together as an enhanced perception of the visual media. A media composer can manipulate this combined audio and visual experience to improve the communication.

Whether dealing with traditional or interactive media, the communication experience is delivered through an intellectual property, usually just called a property. People in the media industry use the word "property" to describe a story and its characters. The same property may be expressed (packaged) in many different media. A song is a type of property, as is a movie script, an advertisement, a corporate Web site, a presentation, and a game. For example, the property *Star Wars* is a story with characters. That property has been expressed as books, films, a theme song, toys, videogames, and so on.

Both the entire property and its component parts can be represented by musical themes and identities that associate the music with an image or story element. The audience remembers the linked association and recalls it whenever the visual, story, or music element reappears.

The process works subconsciously and automatically. Title themes, good-guy and bad-guy themes, soothing music pads, rhythmic action music, and intricate counterpoint are all remembered with their associated pictures and recalled instantly. It's somewhat like a helpful computer program that recognizes when you start typing a word that's already in its database memory, such as the name of a person or address, and then fills in the complete word before you finish typing.

## IDS: LOGOS, EARCONS, THEMES, LEITMOTIFS

First, we'll examine musical identities (IDs), and the way that music helps to communicate a property's story, characters, and settings.

## IDENTITIES

When synchronized with visual media and text, music helps establish the identity of the person, product, program, character, organization, or idea that is being represented. Sometimes known as the ID (pronounced eye-DEE), an identity personifies the property element and is sometimes called a personality. The identity can communicate the essence of a property or an aspect of the property, such as a character, story theme, or personification of an object or organization.

Communicating an essence with words can be difficult and incomplete; communicating an essence with music and images can often be more effective. If a picture is worth a thousand words, how much is the music worth? It can be a significant sum, based on the commissioning (composing) fee and royalties paid to composers who create musical identities. In a TV commercial, the commissioning fee for a musical identity can be tens of thousands of dollars, with additional royalties each time the musical ID is used in a different commercial.

In trying to understand and compose musical identities, it's useful to think of the things that help describe your own identity. Your birth certificate, your driver's license, your school report cards, your annual reviews at work, as well as your bank and credit-card statements, all contain information about who you are, what you do, where you do it, and when. If someone asked your friends and associates about the type of person you are, the characteristics they would relate would also help define your identity.

Musical identities can do the same—impart information and emotions about the who, what, where, when, and why of a property or aspect of a property.

Music identities come in a variety of shapes and sizes, each tailored to fit an appropriate musical length and use.

## Logos

A short musical ID is frequently called a logo—the same word used for graphical and text identities. For example, the musical logo used in the Intel microprocessor ads is well known to radio, television, and Web audiences. Those ascending fourth and fifth intervals, starting from the same base note, form a classic logo: a short musical sequence that is immediately recognized and associated with a product.

Austrian composer Walter Werzowa was living in L.A. when his friend Kyle Cooper was commissioned to create an ad for Intel and asked him to compose the three-second music logo. The ad agency wanted "tones that evoked innovation, trouble-shooting skills, and the inside of a computer, while also sounding corporate and inviting."

How do you do that? Werzowa sat in his home studio for a weekend, trying to come up with the perfect musical phrase. He stared at the four syllables in the words In-tel In-side and started to sing four notes. He used fourths and fifths, because they're the most common intervals worldwide. Perfect intervals for a perfect computer. (You can listen to the Intel logo at http://www.whitwell. ndo.co.uk/musicthing/sounds/intel.mp3.) It took him ten days to record the logo, using more than forty layers of synth tracks to create the unique sound, including a DX7, an Oberheim OBX, a Prophet VS, an Emulator IIIx, a Roland S760, and his beloved Jupiter 8. He used lots of marimba and xylophone sounds because he thinks they sound corporate.

Although he didn't make a fortune on the creative fee, the success of his logo catapulted his career, and he was soon employing a dozen people to manage his composing workload. Intel has since spent more than one billion dollars promoting the sound he created in his home studio. It's played once every five minutes somewhere around the world.

## EXERCISE 3.1. COMPOSE A MUSICAL LOGO

A manufacturer of kitchen appliances that can be connected to the Internet for automated control has an informational Web site to market its products.

The manufacturer's marketing department has created a brand information sheet to define the personality that the company wishes to convey. It includes:

- target audience 1: young working couples moving into their first apartment or house

- target audience 2: middle-age couples remodeling their kitchens

- technology-friendlies who are "with it" and trend conscious

- efficiency-minded people who value saving time by controlling, monitoring, and automating their kitchen appliances from work or from their home offices

**Fig. 3.1.** Visual Logo for Kitchen Appliance Company

1. Compose a musical logo that will play every time a visitor enters the manufacturer's Web site home page.
2. Name it **LogoAppliance.wav,** and save it in your **Demo-Music** disk folder, in a new subfolder named **Logos**.

## Earcons

The term "earcon" was coined by University of Toronto professor Bill Buxton, formerly with Xerox Research and Alias Waveframe. An earcon is an audio logo that's attached to a graphical icon— the visual image used to represent a thing or idea on a screen or printed page. The trash basket image in Windows or Mac operating systems is an example of an icon. The associated sound of waste being emptied when you empty the trash is an earcon. Earcons can be sound effects, music, or a combination of both.

Some earcons for Mac and Windows operating systems are included on the CD in the folder **03_Identities**.

## EXERCISE 3.2. COMPOSE A SET OF EARCONS

1. Compose the following set of earcons for a PIM (personal information manager) device such as a Palm Pilot.

   • Calendar
   • Addresses
   • Notes
   • Applications
   • Sync to a Computer

2. Call these earcons **CalendarEarcon.wav, AddressesEarcon. wav, NotesEarcon.wav, ApplicationsEarcon.wav, and ComputerSyncEarcon.wav**, and save them in a new subfolder named **Earcons**, within your **DemoMusic** folder.

## Themes

When the musical identity is longer than a logo, it's usually called a theme. Themes most frequently are identifiable melodies and sometimes include harmony, rhythm, and/or orchestration. Some themes are just a few notes, like John Williams' shark theme from the movie *Jaws*.

The difference between a short musical theme and a musical logo is somewhat context-dependent. If a very short theme is used for an advertisement, it's usually called a logo. If it's used within a narrative property, the term theme is used, even if the music is very short.

Most themes are longer than a few notes. Sometimes, a theme can be a complete song. John Williams' "Main Title Theme" from *Star Wars* is a typical song-format theme, with A and B melodies and then a recapitulation of the A melody. This is in contrast to his *Jaws* theme noted above, which has just a few notes.

Of course, themes can be intermediate in length between a few notes and a full song. As long as the audience recognizes the musical chunk and associates it with the property or an aspect of the property, it is called a theme.

A theme, in this sense, need not be a melody. It can be a drumbeat or even an ambient pad, provided it is clearly distinguishable by the audience. As an example, listen to **UrgencyTheme.wav** in the **03_Identities** folder.

Media composers frequently compose themes from which they can extract thematic fragments—short portions of the full theme that are recognizable and can be used in the soundtrack to remind the audience of the full theme. An example is the *City-Pulse* television news theme that I wrote with David Hoffert. The file for that theme, **CityPulse.wav**, along with an excerpt from it that's used as an independent music cue, **CityPulseExcerpt.wav**, can be found on the included CD in the folder **03_Identities**.

When you go to a Web site, presentation, or game splash page (a first page that requires user interaction to proceed), you will usually hear a musical theme that is identified with the property. My Web site splash page, http://www.paulhoffert.ca, uses the music theme from a television soundtrack I composed.

One of my favorite media themes is from the *Legend of Zelda* videogame series, composed by Koji Konda. Konda is one of the fathers of videogame music scoring, the composer of the well-known *Super Mario* music themes. The main *Legend of Zelda* theme consists of an easily identified melody, a stirring harmonic pattern, and an action-march rhythm in 4/4 meter with a 12/8 feel implied by triplets. It embodies the essence of the "Quest to Save the Princess." The music provides much of the lead character's nobility, heroics, and action attributes. If you turn off the sound and just watch the screen action, you'll notice that these character attributes are much less obvious without the music.

You can listen to many versions of the *Legend of Zelda Theme,* such as a good dance mix at http://www.angelfire.com/games2/ zorasdomain/zeldamix.mid.

## EXERCISE 3.3. COMPOSE A THEME

A local television station is looking for a music theme for a news-magazine program called *What's Up and What's Going Down.* They will also use the theme in PowerPoint presentations to prospective advertisers, for general promotion of the station, and in interactive kiosks around town. They want several versions of the theme, each orchestrated differently, to be used for various purposes as needs arise.

Compose a theme and orchestrate it into four different versions for use as:

1. The television program theme: 10–20 seconds. Name it **TVtheme.wav**.
2. Full loopable theme, about two minutes, for kiosks and presentation opening splash slide. Name it **TVloop.wav**.
3. Sad version for disaster stories and such. Name it **TVsad. wav**.
4. Upbeat version for entertainment stories. Name it **TVup-beat.wav**.
5. Save the themes in a new subfolder named **Themes**, within your **DemoMusic** folder.

### Leitmotifs

When a theme is associated with a character in a story, it can be woven throughout the soundtrack whenever the character appears onscreen or has some significance to the scene. Composer Richard Wagner used this technique extensively in his nineteenth-century operas, and so the German name for this recurring musical theme—leitmotif (LITE-mo-TEEF)—has become part of theater and film vocabulary. Leitmotifs work just as well in interactive media and are very common in games.

Leitmotifs were popular with media composers in the 1930s and 1940s, when European composers such as Erich Korngold, composer of soundtracks for *The Adventures of Robin Hood*, *Sea Hawk*, and *Captain Blood*, were brought to Hollywood to add their grand orchestral and operatic-like scores to movies. They brought classical musical tools such as leitmotifs to soundtracks, and many of these have become music composition staples since then. Academy Award–winning composers Jerry Goldsmith and Howard Shore have been great proponents of leitmotifs as well, and most media composers use them—particularly when a property has clear characters, as in good-guy/bad-guy movies.

## EXERCISE 3.4. COMPOSE TWO VIDEOGAME LEITMOTIFS

A videogame developer is interested in hiring a composer for a character-based game. The creative team leader puts out a call for composer theme demos of leitmotifs for two key characters:

- a bad-guy monster

- a heroine who successfully slays bad-guys but is compassionate and helps the meek

1. Compose and demo the two themes.
2. Save them as **BadMonster.wav** and **Heroine.wav** in your **DemoMusic** folder, in the **Themes** subfolder.

Listen to the examples **XBadMonster.wav** and **XHeroine.wav** on the included CD in the folder **03_Identities**.

Here's the notation of the XBadMonster leitmotif:

**Fig. 3.2.** Bad Monster Motif

Note the sinister and repeating timpani motif for the bad monster, and the odd rhythm (7/4) that emphasizes the monster's abnormality.

Here's the notation of the XHeroine leitmotif:

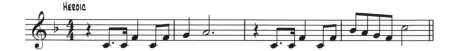

**Fig. 3.3.** Heroine Leitmotif

Note the strong march-like rhythm and major key for the heroine leitmotif.

Chances are that you approached composing your leitmotifs differently. That's to be expected. There is no single approach that's correct when you compose music. Different composers find different solutions to the same musical problems, and the same composer will find different solutions on different days. That's why it's common to compose several demos of a theme, each with different approaches, so you can listen to and discuss them with your clients.

Now, let's discuss how music can help users orient themselves in interactive media.

## MUSIC AS A NAVIGATION AID

Navigating through interactive media's pages, screens, and scenarios can be confusing. It's not always evident how you can get back to a previous screen or at what level you're on in the interactive branching tree. Music can serve as an important navigational aid because users associate it with their position in the interactive flow. Music can be used effectively in this way for presentations, Web sites, games, and other interactive media.

A project I directed at CulTech Research Centre, York University, is a good illustration of how music can assist in interactive navigation. I designed a user interface for a connected community trial in which one hundred homes in Newmarket, Ontario, were provided with interactive hardware and software for entertainment, learning, and socialization. Every home in the neighborhood was given video telephones, computers, and a very high-speed network—15 mb/sec in and out. The purpose was to see if and how people's lives might be affected by the network and content, which included networked healthcare, educational courses, music, and CD-ROMs in an interactive environment.

The interface is designed to use music for navigation in addition to the usual text and visual images. This allows sight-impaired users to navigate the content using musical cues. It works like this:

With no more than six navigational choices onscreen at a time, a user can select from more than a thousand different Web pages using only one or two mouse clicks. The first level of choices—in this case Entertainment, Shop, Learn, Health, Sports, and Community—are rollovers. When the mouse rolls over one of these icon choices, a musical logo sounds and the other five rollovers vanish. At the same time, six new sub-choices appear. If the chosen rollover is Entertainment, for example, the sub-choices that appear are Movies, Theater, Clubs, Concerts, Festivals, and Galleries.

Clicking the mouse on any one of these icons chooses one of the thirty-six options offered so far. The thirty-six options arise from the six secondary choices available from each of the six primary ones (6 x 6 = 36). Let's say you choose Movies as your secondary option. A new set of six rollover icons appears and, if necessary, additional sets of click choices. The total number of choices can be as high as 1,296: 36 for the first click choice x 36 for the second click choice.

This is much easier to see and do than to explain. Play the video named **ManyChoicesFewClicks.mp4** in the enclosed CD to see how it works.

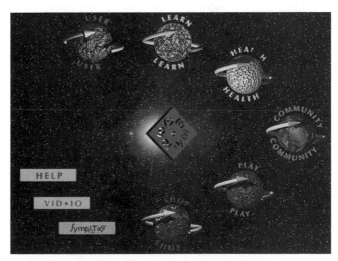

**Fig. 3.4.** 1,296 Choices : Visual + Text + Music Logos

In order to indicate the user's position in the interactivity page branch, I composed a series of musical logos and identities. For the primary choice level, I used six different musical instrument sounds playing a single note and assigned each to one of the roll-overs. Identifying the instrument sound lets you know which option you've chosen. On the second choice level, I composed a short melodic logo made up of a three-note arpeggio. This allows the user to immediately distinguish the main category from the sub-category by the length of the musical sound (one note for the first level; three notes for the second level).

For the last two choice levels, I added more notes to each melody, plus harmony and rhythm. Thus, 1,296 short musical IDs are each linked to the same number of possible rollover and mouse click choices. The result is that users immediately can tell which category and level they're on by listening to the music logo.

Although the described interface was part of a research trial, the principles are useful in everyday interactive music composition. If one thousand choices seems like more than you will ever have to deal with, you haven't analyzed a flow chart for a videogame. As we noted in chapter 1, the number of possible narrative paths increases exponentially with each interactive branch. And videogames have plenty of interactive branches.

Although I had to create 1,296 separate music files for this interface, my compositions only required a small number of creative decisions: choosing the notes for the logo, the instrument sounds, and so on. As we'll learn later in this book, today's powerful computer and console game processors allow composers to add or subtract layers of music tracks and to manipulate them with pitch and tempo changes. This means a composer can specify many different musical cue outcomes based on screen action and user interaction, while providing a much smaller number of music files.

Even when music isn't consciously used for navigational design, it functions that way. If you play an arcade or console videogame enough times, you will soon associate the different music cues with characters, scenarios, and levels. Experienced videogame players can usually tell another player's level and scene of play, just by listening to the music soundtrack.

## WHAT'S NEXT?

Now that we've discussed the basic building blocks of interactive music composition, we'll explore how these can be crafted into soundtracks. The next chapter details musical functions in interactive content. You might be surprised at how extensively composers can use music to manipulate their audiences.

CHAPTER **4**

# FUNCTIONAL MUSIC

Music can be functional. It's used for encouraging good harvests, consecrating marriages, driving out evil spirits, going to war, and dancing at raves. Music adds narrative and emotional depth that are impossible to achieve without it. Interactive media music also serves a wide range of functions, enhancing the content it supports.

## COMPOSING TECHNIQUES

A cue is a named music sequence saved as an audio file. Every project can be divided into music cues, each of which relates to a scene. A scene can be a Web page, a presentation slide, or a segment of a videogame. Before composing a cue for a scene, composers ask the following questions:

## WHAT IS THE OBJECTIVE OF THE SCENE?

The first question quickly separates the professionals from the wannabes. To successfully compose music for a presentation, Web site, game, or mobile platform, you have to understand what goes through the minds of the creators of these media contents. It's no different than film composers needing to understand screen-writing and directing in order to help these creators achieve their objectives in a scene.

To help understand a scene, think of why the content creators made it. Each scenic element was added to help communicate a story, information, or emotional point to the audience. So ... what do you think the desired effect of the combination of elements is?

## HOW CAN MUSIC HELP ACHIEVE THAT OBJECTIVE?

If a scene maximally achieves its objective without music, it doesn't need a music cue. In most cases, a composer is hired because the objectives of the scene creator can be better achieved with music. If you immediately sense how music can help achieve the scene's objective, don't hesitate. Get your pencil or sequencer and start writing. If the answer isn't so obvious, continue with the following questions.

## WHAT ARE THE STRENGTHS OF THE SCENE?

Analyze the elements that make up the scene. Which are the important ones? How can music support or augment the scene's strongest elements?

## WHAT ARE THE WEAKNESSES OF THE SCENE?

How can music disguise or overcome the scene's weaker elements? You can strengthen weak elements and add new music elements that will distract the audience's attention from the scene's weaknesses, using the functional techniques discussed in this chapter.

## STEPS TO COMPOSING

Although every composer has a unique way of creating, most composers use these techniques:

1. Be in touch with your gut feelings.
2. Analyze the functional requirements of the music.
3. Check out how music is used in similar projects.
4. Get on with the job.

Use these techniques to help you compose music in this chapter's exercises.

## FUNCTIONAL MUSIC HELPS TELL A STORY

Music is functional for interactive content. It does more than just entertain. When coupled with images, music influences the way we perceive them, and adds value to the audience's audio-visual experience. A good media composer can manipulate the user's experience by using specific musical functions that include:

- drama

- action

- humor

- characterization

- narrative

- setting

- ambiance

## PREVIEWING MUSIC AND IMAGES TOGETHER

In our exercises, it hasn't been necessary thus far to synchronize music with video files, but some exercises in this chapter require it. In order to preview music and videos together in synchronization, you need the videos to be in a format that can be imported into your sequencer. The most popular video formats on computers are QuickTime and Windows Media, which can both be used with Mac, Windows, and other operating systems.

Your sequencer, provided it has video playback and sync (synchronization) capability, is the most convenient tool for previewing (auditioning) how music works with a scene or screen. The most popular sequencers (Logic, Cubase, Digital Performer) have this feature. All you need to do is import the video file according to the directions in your sequencer's manual, specify a point in the music sequence (measure and beat) that you'd like to synchronize with a point in the video (usually the start), and then press Play. The music and video will start together and let you audition how the music and images work together.

You can easily stop the playback, make changes to the music tracks, and evaluate how the changed music works with the picture. You can alter the music's style, complexity, melody, rhythm, pads, secondary lines, vocals, loop sizes, volume changes, etc.

If you don't have a sequencer with video syncing capability, you can do a rudimentary preview in QuickTime or Windows Media applications. Using this method, you must first open the video file into QuickTime or Windows Media. Then you must export the music sequence that you want to preview from your sequencer, as an audio file. Lastly, you must import this file into the QuickTime or Windows Media video file as an overlay audio track. This method is more complicated and may require paying an upgrade fee for a pro version of QuickTime or Windows Media, since the free playback applications usually do not support this type of audio import. Consult your QuickTime or Windows Media manual if you use this method, since different versions of these programs have different capabilities and instructions.

## DRAMA

Music is frequently used to heighten the drama or emotional content of a scene. Music can make a scary scene more horrific, a love scene more romantic, and a tense scene more edgy. It can create suspense if the screen images lack it. It can impute good and evil intent to the onscreen characters. It can suggest a relationship between two characters whose actions do not indicate one. Most of all, it can greatly amplify and deepen an audience's emotions. If you don't appreciate how large a role music plays in dramatization, just rent some horror, action, and romance movies and some videogames. Watch key scenes with the sound turned off, then again with the sound on, and you'll quickly gain respect for how much emotional emphasis the music adds.

Music is such a powerful dramatic tool that it must be used carefully, so as not to overwhelm the visual images. There is a great range between subtle dramatic enhancement and over-the-top melodramatic musical treatments. The composer must decide which stylistic approach is appropriate for each property, based on the styles of the other creative elements. These include the directorial and acting approaches, the producer's creative vision, the art direction, and the cinematography. These can range in style from subtle to smack-you-in-the-back-of-the-head, from serious to campy, and from muted emotions to visceral and stirring impacts. A composer must choose the stylistic approach that fits best with the styles of the other elements and team members.

In the early days of Hollywood movies, a music dramatization technique called foreshadowing was frequently used. If a bad guy was about enter a room, you would hear "bad guy" music a few seconds before he came through the door. This set the scene in advance for the evil to come. Nowadays, this style is out of fashion in serious films because it sounds corny and can evoke a comedic rather than dramatic response. Of course, you can use foreshadowing to very good effect in a comedy.

## EXERCISE 4.1. SCORE A DRAMATIC SCENE

1. Locate the video file **DramaticScene.mov** in the **04_ Functions** folder on your included CD, and load it into your sequencer. See your sequencer manual for instructions if you need them.
2. Play the video scene silently many times until you understand its dramatic intent.
3. Compose music for the scene. Save your cue as **Dramatic1.wav** in a new subfolder named **Functions** within your **DemoMusic** folder.
4. Synchronize your music score with the video. Check your sequencer manual, if necessary.
5. Listen carefully to how your score helps or hurts the scene.
6. Score the scene again, this time with a different musical approach. Name the file **Dramatic2.wav.**
7. Load the music file **DramaticMusic.wav** from the **04_Functions** folder on the CD into your sequencer, and sync it up with the scene.
8. Note the differences in how the scene plays using each of your two cues and the original music cue.
9. Compare the effectiveness of your two approaches with the original score.

## ACTION

Action scenes are major beneficiaries of added musical excitement, although music can also add excitement to scenes without much action. Examples of the former might be a raft going over rapids or a gunfight. An example of the latter might be a role-playing game in which an onscreen character prepares for a fight by the player choosing the type of weapon, attack, and defense strength. In the second case, there might be no action occurring onscreen (it might even be a text screen), but the music must nonetheless convey a sense of action and excitement. In a business presentation, music could add excitement and imply action for a slide whose text reads, "Next Quarter, We're Going to Rout the Competition."

Pulses beat more rapidly when people are excited, because the heart needs to deliver more blood to muscles that are preparing for action. The tempo of music also has an effect on heart rate: your pulse slows or quickens in accordance with the tempo of the music you're listening to. The background music at your dentist's office likely will be soft ballads or slower classical movements to relax your pulse, while the music at a dance club will be up-tempo, elevating your heart rate appropriately to prepare you for the physical activity on the dance floor.

Since musical tempos are related to heart rate, it makes sense to use faster tempos when onscreen characters' heart rates rise because they're excited or in the midst of action. Consequently, action scenes mostly use up-tempo music, frequently with hot jazz or rock rhythms.

Action scenes don't always require exciting music. Sometimes the onscreen action is intense but moderate in pace, such as a character diffusing a bomb, or a thief sneaking around a building. In the first case, a clocklike percussion sound using a moderate tempo might work to conjure up the tension of time ticking by. In the second, a high, stringy pad with irregular percussion might indicate the unexpected nature of what's coming next.

Creative composers sometimes "play against type" by using music that counterpoints the visual images. It's worth renting the Academy Award-winning movie *Chariots of Fire* to check out the racing scene. Composer Vangelis scored this scene with a slow-motion synth cue that emphasizes the mental state of the runner rather than his action of racing.

Sound effects can have an important impact on how a composer scores an action scene. Since music and sound effects are combined in the final soundtrack mix, composers need to treat sound effects like additional instruments in the orchestration. Sometimes, the implications are minimal. Other times, the sound effects can compete with the music, and the impacts of both are diminished. That's why it's important for composers to collaborate with the sound-effects team, to ensure that all efforts are maximized and pay off in the final audio mix.

Action sequences are particularly prone to this clash of music and effects because they usually are filled with lots of heavy, low-frequency sound effects (bombs, car engines, waterfalls) and intrusive percussive sounds (gunshots, punches). Experienced composers usually leave "room" for these effects so that the music and sound effects both can be mixed at high volumes without interfering with each other.

One technique that composers use when there are lots of percussive sound effects is to emphasize slower elements in the score, such as melodies, letting the sound effects provide some of the rhythm in the mixed soundtrack. Another technique, used when there are continuous low-frequency sounds like machinery or engine rumbles, is to be more selective in using low frequency instruments like basses, tubas, or timpani so that they aren't "washed out" by the effects.

## EXERCISE 4.2. SCORE AN ACTION SCENE

1. Locate the video file **ActionScene.mov** in the folder **04_Functions** on your included CD and load it into your sequencer.
2. Play the video scene silently many times until you understand its dramatic intent.
3. Score the scene. Name the file **Action1.wav**, and save it in the **Functions** subfolder within your **DemoMusic** folder.
4. Synchronize your music score with the video. Check your sequencer manual, if necessary.
5. Listen carefully to how your score helps or hurts the scene.
6. Score the scene again, this time with a different musical approach. Name the file **Action02.wav** and save it in your **DemoMusic** folder.
7. Load the music file **ActionMusic.wav** from the **04_Functions** folder on the CD into your sequencer and sync it up with the scene. Is it more or less effective than your music score?
8. Note the differences in how the scene plays using each of your two scores and the original music score.
9. Compare the effectiveness of your two approaches with the original score.

# HUMOR

Humor can be heightened or created by appropriate music. A silent animation of a monkey swinging from tree to tree may be interesting, but if you couple it with a quirky bassoon, xylophone, and a staccato flute passage, it can become cute and funny. Listen to the example on the included CD, **xylohumor.wav** in the **04_Functions** folder.

Humor can be tricky to score. You first need to understand what's funny about a scene—what the setup and payoff are—before you can use music to add to the scene's humor. Generally, the setup prepares the audience for the joke, like a comedian's "straight line" setting up the "punch line." If the music gives away the joke too soon, the punch line may not have its maximal impact. Think of a character tiptoeing up to a door, but at the last minute knocking over a vase, accompanied by a loud crash. A composer might score the setup with sparse and quiet suspense music, which would set up the anticipation of the payoff of the loud crash.

Some scenes are humorous without having a specific setup and payoff, such as characters chasing each other while engaged in broad comedic gestures. In this case, a composer might just go with the flow and underline the onscreen mayhem. **FunnyChase.wav** in the folder **04_Functions** is such a cue.

There are many types of humor, and each requires its own unique musical approach.

A parody imitates a person or event in a humorous way. It's also known as mimicry, a lampoon, spoof, send-up, mockery, takeoff, burlesque, travesty, or charade. If the person or event that is being parodied can be associated with music, then that music or a "parody" of that music is effective in drawing the comparison and strengthening the humor. For example, the series of *Scary Movie* comedy films parody the horror genre, using melodramatic music to amplify the humor of the funny scenes.

Satire ridicules and attacks human follies and vices using irony, derision, and wit. *The Simpsons* and *M\*A\*S\*H* are examples of satiric content. Each of these uses a different musical approach. Composer Alf Clausen uses a combination of wacky musical treatments, accurate knock-offs of popular songs, and dramatic cues to make *The Simpsons* episodes zing. Johnny Mandel, composer of the theme music for both the *M\*A\*S\*H* movie and television series, targeted the psychological aspects of the story. The original lyric, written by director Robert Altman's son Mike, is about suicide—hardly a funny topic, but a great counterpoint to the comedic situations, and a comment on the inanity of war.

Satire frequently exposes the incongruity between something that is expected to happen and what actually happens, particularly when the result is absurd or laughable. Since the outcome is unexpected, music can set up the humor by suggesting the expected outcome, accentuating the surprise of the unexpected outcome.

Physical humor was honed to a fine art with the early silent films, which relied on pratfalls (embarrassing and humiliating trip-ups, falls, and such) and dangerous situations, such as Buster Keaton hanging from the hands of a giant clock on a skyscraper. Perhaps the king of physical humor today is Jim Carrey, whose physical contortions produce belly laughs across cultural and linguistic barriers. Physical humor is usually accompanied by funny music, often with instruments used as sound effects. This type of music is used in the early Jim Carrey movies, such as *Ace Ventura: Pet Detective*, with a soundtrack by Ira Newborn.

Tension-and-release humor sets up a suspenseful situation whose release is triggered by one of the humorous forms. Music plays a critical role in creating tension. An example is the *Roadrunner* cartoon, in which Wile E. Coyote tiptoes gingerly, accompanied by pizzicato strings, to set up and ambush the Roadrunner bird, and then gets struck by some calamitous object (anvil, bomb, you name it). Note the use of silence (bar 2 and bar 4) to increase suspense, and the diminished chord at bar 5 to enhance the visual payoff.

**Fig. 4.1.** Tension and Release Music

A good way to learn how to score humor is to watch cartoons. Cartoons rely almost exclusively on music to flush out the characters and create the cadence (emotional curve) for making the humor pay. Comedy movies offer another valuable learning opportunity; analyze how each music score is used effectively and, sometimes, not so. In fact, watching rented movies and television programs works for learning about all types of music scoring. When you critically watch a film, make sure you learn from soundtracks that don't work well as well as those that do.

## EXERCISE 4.3. SCORE A HUMOROUS SCENE

1. Locate the video file **HumorScene.mov** in the folder **04_Functions** on your included CD, and load it into your sequencer. See your sequencer manual for instructions if you need them.
2. Play the video scene silently many times until you understand its dramatic intent.
3. Score the scene. Name the file **Humor1.wav**, and save it in the **Functions** subfolder within your **DemoMusic** folder.
4. Synchronize your music score with the video. Check your sequencer manual, if necessary.
5. Listen carefully to how your score helps or hurts the scene.
6. Score the scene again, this time with a different musical approach. Name the file **Humor2.wav**, and save it in the **Functions** subfolder within your **DemoMusic** folder.
7. Load the music file **HumorMusic.wav** from the **04_ Functions** folder on the CD into your sequencer and sync it up with the scene.
8. Note the differences in how the scene plays using each of your two scores and the original music score.
9. Compare the effectiveness of your two approaches with the original score.

## CHARACTERIZATION

Music themes can depict human character traits, and, once they are tied to a character, can connect that character to a scene or shot.

Character traits define personality. They are very helpful in discussing and focusing the objectives of a functional music theme or leitmotif. Terms like courageous and adventuresome depict a different type of personality than terms like careful, dreamy, and thoughtful, for example. A talkative, outgoing, and friendly person is very different than a shy and withdrawn one, and the music that characterizes such people would be different, too.

When you connect a musical theme, leitmotif, or orchestration to a character, the audience links the two in memory and associates them. This allows composers to imply the presence or thoughts of a character even if he or she is not present onscreen. The classic example is in the movie *Laura*, whose music score won an Academy Award for composer David Raksin. The title theme is associated with the character Laura, who is murdered. The theme is used throughout the movie to imply Laura's relevance to a scene, even when she's not present. It's worth renting this movie to check out the score, particularly if you're into film noir.

Like good magicians, film and television composers use this trick of association and misdirection to create illusions without the audience ever suspecting that it is being manipulated. A classic example is John Williams' use of the shark theme in the movie *Jaws*. All that's needed are a few notes of his low-pitched shark theme to evoke the terror associated with the shark. This is another example of effectively using music to counterpoint (be contrary to) the onscreen image. The audience experiences the conflict between the idyllic visual and horrific music and chooses to relate to the musical statement over the visual. The message of fear is conveyed more strongly because of the contrast.

Character indication is particularly important in role-playing games, in which the point of view (POV) of the camera is frequently that of the character associated with the game player.

The following adjectives are helpful in defining the character traits that you may wish to portray musically.

| | | | |
|---|---|---|---|
| absentminded | energetic | macho | sexy |
| adventurous | evil | mean | shiftless |
| ambitious | expert | messy | short |
| angry | fearful | mischievous | shrewd |
| awkward | fierce | nagging | shy |
| boastful | flexible | neat | sly |
| bold | forgetful | obedient | smart |
| bossy | forgiving | organized | sneaky |
| brave | friendly | outspoken | softhearted |
| bright | fun-loving | patient | spunky |
| busy | fussy | patriotic | stingy |
| calm | generous | persistent | stubborn |
| carefree | gentle | playful | studious |
| careless | gloomy | pleasant | successful |
| caring | greedy | polite | superstitious |
| cautious | gullible | poor | suspicious |
| changeable | handsome | prideful | talkative |
| charming | happy | proud | tall |
| cheerful | hardworking | quarrelsome | thoughtful |
| clever | helpful | quick-tempered | timid |
| combative | heroic | quiet | tough |
| commanding | honest | reasonable | trusting |
| conceited | humble | reckless | understanding |
| confused | humorous | relaxed | unfriendly |
| considerate | imaginative | resourceful | unkind |
| contented | independent | respectful | unselfish |
| cooperative | integrity | responsible | wild |
| courageous | intelligent | restless | wise |
| cowardly | inventive | rich | withdrawn |
| creative | jealous | romantic | witty |
| cruel | jolly | rude | |
| curious | joyful | sad | |
| dainty | keen | sadistic | |
| daring | kind | secretive | |
| demanding | lazy | self-centered | |
| dependable | lighthearted | self-confident | |
| determined | loud | selfish | |
| disagreeable | lovable | sensitive | |
| dreamy | loving | sentimental | |
| dull | loyal | serious | |

Carefully watch scenes with characters in them, and select traits from the list (or better ones if you come up with them) that you think describe the characters. Then discuss your planned musical characterizations with your client and production team members to make sure you're all on the same page. You may be surprised to find out that the screenwriter and director intended a character to have traits that didn't come across to you.

## EXERCISE 4.4. COMPOSE A CHARACTER THEME

1. Choose two to four traits from the list above, and compose a theme that portrays a character with a combination of those traits.
2. Name your theme **Character.wav**, and save it to the **Functions** subfolder in your **DemoMusic** folder.
3. Make a cassette or CD copy.
4. Play your theme for some friends, and see if they can guess what traits you're trying to portray. Ask them which traits your music brings to their minds.
5. If you haven't been successful in conveying your character musically, analyze which musical elements led your audience in a different direction. Change the problematic musical elements and see if a new group of friends gets your musical characterizations.

## NARRATIVE

Narrative elements help tell a story or convey a message. Like other musical functions, narrative elements can be conveyed through music without occurring onscreen. To be effective in this manner, a music cue needs to be associated in the audience's mind with the narrative element. For example, the music associated with Clark Kent's transformation into Superman, while he ducks into a phone booth to change into his Superman costume, is enough to indicate his transformation. We needn't actually see him changing onscreen to get the picture. The same can apply for any recurring narrative event. Link it once with music, and you can evoke the event subsequently by using that music in another cue.

Some music is already associated in the audience's mind with story or message elements. These can be immediately suggested by using the music, without first setting up the association. For example, a national anthem is associated with a country and also with citizens of that country. Use an anthem and you can bring to mind a character of that nationality.

Songs can be used effectively to move the narrative forward because they contribute both a musical function and a lyric, which tells the story with words, like dialog. The advent of video-game platforms that can play audio files from CDs and DVDs was an impetus for licensing songs into interactive media. These help tell stories and convey messages with strong emotional connection to the players.

"We Are the Champions" by Queen is an example of a song whose lyrics and anthem-like quality make it ideal for use in presentations and videogames, when the message is that an organization, team, or army has proven victorious. It's a very popular song for this type of use.

Mobile phones have featured music from the outset—first as ringtones, without lyrics, then as mastertunes (song excerpts), and recently as complete songs. Although the screen size of mobile platforms is limited, the sound quality can be very good (see chapter 9, "Mobile Media Music"). Consequently, instrumental music and songs are expected to be important content for mobile platforms, including soundtracks for video content. Music is particularly important as a narrative element on mobile media because the small image size can't convey as much information as larger screens can.

I wrote the song "Song of Freedom" with lyricist Brenda Hoffert for the film *Wild Horse Hank*. The producers wanted to indicate the thoughts of the lead character, a teenage girl who is trying to save a herd of wild horses from being slaughtered. In this scene, she's crossing a desert with the herd and is worried that the horses will die of thirst before they get to pastures and streams on the other side. The song lyric makes it clear that she is determined to bring them to their freedom. Here's a verse and chorus:

*Verse*
Hot sun, blazing in the sky
Desert so endless and so dry
Cool breeze, blow a little breath my way

I've gotta make it
Gotta make it one more day
***Chorus***
I keep hearing the song of freedom blazing in my brain
I keep hearing the sound of the west wind callin' out my name

A short version of the song, **SongOfFreedom.wav**, is on the enclosed CD, in the folder **04_Functions**.

## EXERCISE 4.5. COMPOSE A NARRATIVE SONG

1. Write a song lyric that describes a desperate lover, despondent because the love of his (her) life has been kidnapped and is in imminent danger of being killed. He (she) prays or hopes for a miracle so they can be reunited.
2. Compose music for the lyrics. Write the song in one of the following styles: rock, r&b ballad, or rap/hip-hop.
3. Name the song **SongNarrative.wav**, and save it in a new **Songs** subfolder of your **DemoMusic** folder.

## SETTING: PLACE, TIME, AND CULTURE

Geographic location can be indicated using musical scales, instruments, and orchestras endemic to a location. Examples include pentatonic and quarter-tone scales for the Far East, bagpipes for Scotland or Ireland, square-dance fiddling for American cowboys, and the sitar for India.

The choice of instrumentation, orchestration, and style can steer the audience to the specific time period of the property. A diatonic harp evokes Biblical eras, serpents and crumhorns suggest Shakespearean times, a harpsichord reminds us of the Baroque period, and large lush orchestrations evoke the Romantic era. Folk-rock points to the 1960s, hard rock suggests the 1970s, power-pop focuses on the 1980s, and hip-hop recalls the 1990s.

Every culture has its emblematic music. Music in 5/8 and 7/8 meters connect us to Greece, reggae's free-floating bass lines and guitar strums on the second and fourth beats of each bar connect it to the West Indian community, and gospel music's full-fisted stride piano playing is an unmistakable identity for African-American culture in the early twentieth century.

With the advent of globalization, cross-culturalism, and world music, however, the direct link between a cultural music style and its community is less unique. Nowadays, we frequently transplant musical styles from one place and culture to another. Djembe drums and tablas, for example, once evoked African and Indian cultures, but today can be heard as part of rhythm sections in mainstream pop and film music.

## EXERCISE 4.6. EVOKE A SETTING

1. Research authentic instruments used in Middle Eastern music.
2. Research scales and melodies used in Middle Eastern music.
3. Find synth or sample sounds that resemble authentic Middle Eastern instruments.
4. Compose a piece of music that evokes Arabian culture. Name it **Arabian.wav**, and save it in the **Functions** subfolder of your **DemoMusic** folder.

The best strategy for ensuring that your ideas for the musical setting are in tune with the project is to discuss them with your producer or team leader, and then test a cue idea by mocking it up and syncing it with the screen images, using the sequencer-syncing techniques discussed in the previous chapter.

## ATMOSPHERE

The music functions detailed above work best with scenes that need to convey a story or information. Sometimes, the most important role that music can play is to indicate a general mood or ambiance, setting the environment for the scene and putting the audience in the right frame of mind. For these types of cues, it's less important for the music to mimic onscreen activities than to capture an overall feeling. The flow of the music should knit the scenic elements together, providing cohesion and a sense of unity for the audience.

Atmospheric cues are easy to write for some composers and difficult for others. Songwriters generally find them easier than do dramatic composers, since songwriters are used to working with a single rhythm and repetitive sections rather than with an emotional curve.

Atmospheric cues are very useful in interactive media because of their "accordion" nature; they can easily expand and contract in length. Their evenness makes them relatively easy to edit into loops. In fact, loops of eight bars or less generally yield atmospheric cues when they are repeated. Web sites frequently need this function—a sort of musical wallpaper that can unite disparate elements on a page.

## EXERCISE 4.7. COMPOSE AN AMBIENT TRACK

1. Compose an atmospheric track for a vintage airplane race. Name it **AirRace.wav**, and save it in the **Functions** subfolder of your **DemoDisk** folder.
2. Compose an atmospheric track for a night-time urban street. Name it **Urban.wav**, and save it in the **Functions** subfolder of your **DemoDisk** folder.
3. Compose an atmospheric track for a pastoral setting in a meadow. Name it **Meadow.wav**, and save it in the **Functions** subfolder of your **DemoDisk** folder.

## USING FUNCTIONAL CATEGORIES

The functional categories detailed in this chapter and the musical identity techniques outlined in the previous chapter should get your creative juices flowing to come up with ideas for music cues. They will also help focus your discussions with members of the production team. The analyses and questions will help you understand how the elements of a scene can work together for maximum impact. They are very useful for getting started on a new property, particularly if you're drawing a blank as to how to proceed.

## WHAT'S NEXT?

This chapter concludes part I, "The Basics." Now that we have some techniques and understanding about composing for interactive media, it's time to get practical and walk the walk. The next part explains specific interactive media and discusses how to approach composing for each one. We'll begin with presentations.

Part **II**

# THE MEDIA

CHAPTER

# 5

# PRESENTATIONS

Interactive experiences are usually one-to-one, with a single user controlling the pace and flow of the experience. Presentations are interactive, but, like traditional media, involve one-to-many communications as well. The single presenter controls the pace and flow, but the experience is shared by many in the audience.

## BUSINESS PRESENTATIONS

Composers new to the field often associate interactive media music with consumer activities: videogames, DVDs, and Web sites. But businesses use interactive media much more frequently and are willing to pay for music when it's used for their marketing, promotion, and information activities. In this regard, presentations are by far the largest segment of interactive media use.

Corporate, non-profit, and government organizations provide most of the commercial presentation work for composers. These organizations produce thousands of presentations every day, on every conceivable topic and in every language. Many medium to large organizations have in-house AV (audio-visual) departments that help prepare the presentations given by company employees and executives. These departments create or commission the organization's presentations, DVDs, and videos. Presentations are used in many environments and have many audiences, including:

- employees
- managers
- customers
- shareholders
- the media
- business associates

Music always has been used extensively in corporate videos, but its use in presentations has only recently begun to take off. In the past, presentation music was limited by the insufficient digital storage, processor speed, and audio playback capacity of presentation computers. Since each presentation location might have its own computer and AV equipment, a previous lack of minimum technical standards caused AV departments and presenters to shy away from using music, since it could cause a technical problem at presentation time.

That problem has now been overcome. The advent of modern operating systems such as Windows XP and Mac OS X, along with the powerful computers that run them, allow current computers to reliably play audio and video files and to synchronize these media within presentation programs. The result has been a growing use of music and video materials in presentations, and so the need for well-composed and well-selected music is rapidly increasing. This presents an excellent opportunity for composers.

## STRIPFILMS AND SLIDESHOWS

To understand modern presentation technology, let's first look at how it evolved and what needs it fills. The earliest presentation technology used stripfilms. The "strip" was a roll of 35 mm positive film, drawn through a projector one image at a time by the presenter or an operator. Stripfilms, popular in the 1930s and 1940s, allowed a speaker to use images with a presentation, and to tailor the presentation to the time available and to the specific audience. Music was generally absent from stripfilm presentations.

**Fig. 5.1.** Film Strip Projector (Left), Kodak Carousel Slide Projector (Right)

The next technological development cut apart each image of the stripfilm and mounted it in its own frame: a slide. The projector "slides" each framed image in and out of the light path, inserting a new one while ejecting the previous one. A big advantage of slides over films or stripfilms is that you can rearrange the order of slides in a presentation, allowing a presenter to assemble many different slide shows from a single collection. Slide shows began overtaking stripfilms as a preferred presentation technology in the 1950s. In the 1960s, new technology became available that added synchronized music soundtracks, making slide shows ideal for trade shows and public presentations.

Slide show technology is so convenient and intuitive for presentations that it is still used today, more than fifty years after it was introduced. It is the model on which computer presentation programs are based—individual slides (screens) that can be easily reordered and presented sequentially under the presenter's control.

# PRESENTATION PROGRAMS

PowerPoint, Open Office, and OperaShow are widely used presentation programs for multi-platform environments. There are also presentation programs designed for specific operating systems, such as Keynote for Mac OS, Corel Presentations, Lotus Freelance Graphics, and GoBe Productive for Windows, and KPresenter, MagicPoint, or Pointless for Linux. All of these follow the same basic slideshow framework.

The user creates slides, which in this environment are computer screens with standard landscape proportions (640 x 480, 800 x 600, or 1024 x 768 pixels). Each slide can contain text, still images, music, and video. Then the user arranges the order of the slides and adds transitions, such as dissolves, between slides.

The resulting presentations are much like the slide projector shows that preceded computer presentations. But it's much quicker to make a slide on a computer than to take a picture of a physical scene with a camera, process the film, cut it into individual images, and mount the particular image in a slide holder.

In contrast, presentation programs allow you to easily import text and images from many popular programs or to use sound and image libraries available on CD, DVD, and on the Web. In addition, many presentation programs have tools for creating text, images, and graphs within the program, greatly increasing the author's presentation choices.

Text is usually the backbone of a presentation. Each slide generally has title text and body text. The title summarizes the main point, and the body provides the details. Unlike a normal text document, slides generally don't use sentences or paragraphs, but instead contain information and concepts in an abbreviated text style called "bullet points" or just "bullets." All the bullet points on a slide can appear at once when the slide appears, or they can be brought onto the slide sequentially, when the presenter clicks a mouse or types on a computer keyboard.

Usually, images are created in programs such as Photoshop, while music and sound effects are created in a music sequencer. These media are then imported into a slide and placed where they are desired.

## POWERPOINT MUSIC

By far, the most popular presentation program is PowerPoint by Microsoft. If you want to create music for presentations, you should learn to use it. Almost all other presentation programs can import PowerPoint-formatted files, which have the filename extension "ppt." Once you've mastered it, you'll be able to learn to use other presentation programs relatively easily. PowerPoint is available on Mac OS and Windows platforms.

If you've been asked to create or select music for a PowerPoint presentation, it's fairly straightforward to link musical selections with individual slides. However, controlling how each music cue will synchronize with a slide is not very intuitive in PowerPoint. It requires knowing exactly which menus to access and which options to set. Following is an exercise that illustrates how to attach and synchronize a music file to a presentation slide.

## EXERCISE 5.1. ADDING MUSIC TO A PRESENTATION SLIDE

Most presentation programs allow you to add music tracks to slides and to start their play either manually with a mouse click or key-press, or automatically on a slide change. This and the following presentation exercises are based on Microsoft Power-Point. Refer to the manual of your presentation program if you're using a different one or a different version of PowerPoint.

1. Use a presentation program to open the file named **Presentation1.ppt** from the folder **05_Presentations** on the included CD. This presentation has three slides: a title slide and two subsequent slides with lines of text on them. The box at the lower left, under the slide, toggles the screen among (a) the slide graphic (shown below), (b) a view with accompanying text, (c) a slide-sorting view, and (d) running the finished slide show (the icon of a movie screen). After you complete this exercise, experiment with this simple presentation, removing and adding music files, changing the timing of the music, and so on.

**Fig. 5.2.** Presentation1.ppt, Slide 1

2. Display the opening (sometimes called "Title") slide.
3. On the Insert menu, point to Movies and Sounds. A drop-down menu will appear.
4. If the music you want to use is in the PowerPoint Gallery, select Sound from Gallery.

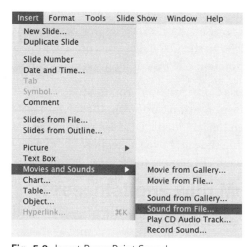

**Fig. 5.3.** Insert PowerPoint Sound

5.  The Sound Gallery lets you audition music and sounds using the Preview checkbox, import music and sounds into the Gallery using the Import button, and insert a music file into a slide using the Insert button. When you preview the music files that come bundled in the PowerPoint Gallery, you'll understand why they are not used very often and why there are jobs for composers like yourself.

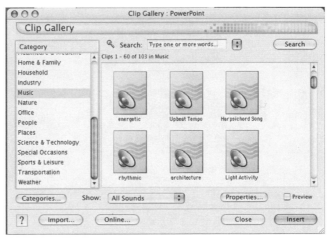

**Fig. 5.4.** Sound Clip Gallery

6.  If you don't want to store your music file or audition it in the Gallery, you can skip step 5 and instead select Music from File. For this exercise, locate and open the music file **Present-Music1.mp3** in **05_Presentations**. You can similarly add a file from a CD by selecting "**Play CD Audio Track**," locating the CD in the dialog box, and double-clicking the music file you want to use. PowerPoint accepts popular sound formats such as MP3, AIFF, WAV, and music CD files.

7.  A sound icon appears on the slide, whether you selected music from the Gallery or a disk. This indicates that there's a music track associated with the slide. Clicking on the sound icon in the slide previews the music.

**Fig. 5.5.** PowerPoint Sound Icon

8.  A dialog box appears, asking if you want the sound to play automatically when you display the slide, or when you click the sound icon during a slide show.

9.  If you want more control over when your music file(s) will play, click on the **Slide Show** menu and pull down to the **Custom Animation** menu item.

**Fig. 5.6.** Selecting Custom Animation

10. The custom animation window box lets you select the object on a slide that you wish to control. In this case, it's the sound object. Then you set the Animation Order and the Effect Options. The Effect Options window and menus let you set the Timing of the sound, set the sound to repeat (loop), rewind to the beginning of the sound file when the next event happens, and so on. Other options are in the Effect and Media Options panes.

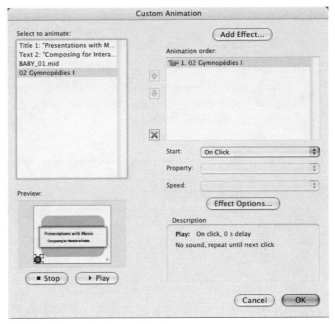

**Fig. 5.7.** Custom Animation Window

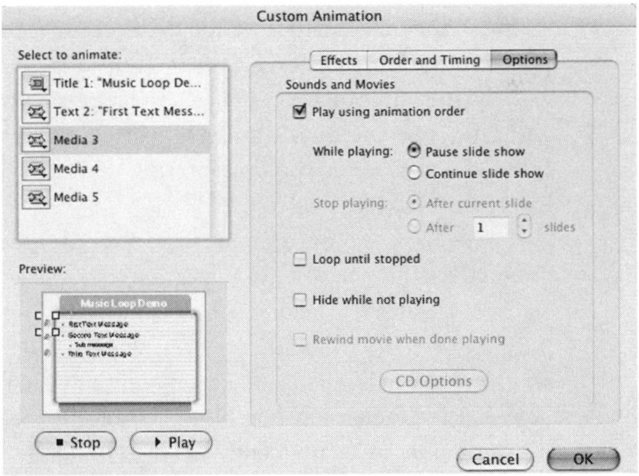

**Fig. 5.8.** Effect Options

### PowerPoint Tips

PowerPoint interprets the Space Bar and Arrow keys on a computer to be the same as a mouse click, so a presenter can move through slide changes and trigger movies and music without using a mouse.

When you're working in PowerPoint, it's helpful to be able to stop a music file, loop, or video when you want to make a change. The Escape (ESC) key usually will stop a presentation and kick you back into the creation mode.

You can play more than a single music or audio file at the same time in PowerPoint. If you want a looped music track with sound effects or dialog playing over the music, PowerPoint can handle it. Just make sure to get your audio levels set right so the mix works. Audio levels can't be set in PowerPoint, but you can open the audio files in your sequencer, set the mix levels there, and then save the adjusted audio files.

# LINEAR VERSUS INTERACTIVE PRESENTATIONS

Presentations come in two flavors. One is linear (fixed length), similar to a movie, and the other is interactive. The environment in which the presentation will be delivered dictates which type of presentation is used. The first type is used in unattended kiosks, usually in public places such as museums and malls. It plays without a presenter and can be triggered by a user or automatically, by a sensor. Or, the presentation can run continuously on a loop, like a repeated video.

In this book, we concentrate on the second type of presentations: interactive. These have a live presenter who speaks as the slides are displayed, gauges the audience's attention and interest, and adjusts the pace of each slide on the fly, even skipping some slides if necessary. The ability to change the total length of the presentation and the length of each individual slide is crucial. Presentations at seminars or conferences frequently need to be longer or shorter than expected because of delays or other unforeseen events.

Experienced presenters are able to sense how their material is going over with their audience—whether the audience is laughing at jokes or dozing off, for example. Presenters are also aware that information in the presentation may have been made available to the audience through handouts or from other presenters. Consequently, they modify the pace of their talk and reapportion time for each slide. The unknown length of each slide drives the need for variable length musical loops and other interactive compositional formats.

## SLIDES = CHAPTERS IN A STORY

Now it's time to get down to the creative part. Composing music for media is about storytelling. A presentation is a type of story. You can think of each slide as a chapter in the story or as a scene in a movie.

Not every slide in a presentation needs music, just as not every scene in a movie needs music. Appropriately placed music heightens the communication of the slide's message; likewise, music in the wrong place can lessen the impact of the message. Composers are hired for our ability to discern between these outcomes and to use our creative judgments to ensure the best possible communications outcome.

Style is a major consideration in deciding what type of music should be used where. Tailor the music and production to fit the audience's sociographic, demographic, and professional makeup. Of course, you also have to take into account the content of the presentation. A presentation about a new line of teen clothing, a presentation for the rollout of a telephone service, and a presentation of experimental results at an academic conference all require very different stylistic treatments. In each case, the presentation content should be well matched to the audience. If the same presentation is planned for different types of audiences, the composer may suggest to the client that several music soundtracks be prepared, tuned to the most accessible musical styles of each audience.

## USING DRAMATIC ARC = TELLING A GOOD STORY

When developing presentations, remember that music should help tell the story. The audience must be engaged at every step along the plot path. The beginning must quickly capture the audience's interest in order to keep them tuned in for the rest of the story. The middle parts should ebb and flow with a combination of information and detail between more interesting highlights. Finally, the story should tie up all the loose ends and build to a satisfying climax.

Although composers can't control how well the presentation creators have told the story in text and visual images, their music can improve the story flow significantly, emphasize the important points, and add interest to the boring bits. The music soundtrack for a presentation or other interactive media can help the storytelling, just like a film soundtrack does.

In literature and screenwriting, the chart of story elements is known as the dramatic arc. In narrative media, a good dramatic arc is very important to convey the message (story) to the audience. Music is the most powerful element in a multimedia production for controlling the dramatic arc, emphasizing some sections and weaving together others.

Presentations, like videogames, are narrative. They tell a story based on a contrived script. Although individual scenes vary within each presentation or game play, the overall emotional arc from beginning to end has been created and controlled by the authors and can be made much more effective by the judicious addition of music.

Experienced presenters know that you should start with a strong attention grabber and build to a strong closing that restates the major points of your presentation. The content in between is negotiable, but, like a good book or movie, usually contains information and details sandwiched between emotional highlights. In a novel, the emotional highlights might be action or love interests. In a presentation, the emotional highlights might contain sneak previews, relevant news, personal experiences, or other topical items that get the audience involved with the presentation.

While every presentation is different, it's common to find revelations of juicy story tidbits, such as new products or new findings, in the first quarter of the presentation. It's also common to have sexy bits, such as humor or video clips, in the last quarter of the presentation, when the audience is most prone to nap.

grabber        juicy bit                              sexy bit    big closer

**Fig. 5.9.** Dramatic Arc of a Presentation

Each presentation, like each novel, will have its own dramatic arc, but elements will be the same.

Since the opening and closing of a presentation need the greatest impact, music usually plays its greatest roles at the beginning and end. Music in the body of a presentation is most likely to be used at the key points, to underscore the juicy bits and sexy bits. The balance of the presentation can work with or without music, depending on the stylistic requirements of the presenter and the presentation environment.

Here are some suggestions.

**Grabber.** This is equivalent to a home page or splash page on the Web, or the opening titles of a movie. This music should set the tone for the entire presentation. The PowerPoint producer can help you with the objective of the presentation and the style that's appropriate for the audience and environment. Does the organization want to portray the message as leading edge? Solid and safe? Light and humorous? Timely? Music can set the stage appropriately.

Use music that will "play" to the audience's inherent biases—styles that they've heard on television, in films, on the radio, or in commercials. If the organization has a musical theme it uses for marketing this message, it's a good idea to incorporate this theme into the grabber.

**Juicy Bits.** These items may be powerful, funny, or otherwise impactful. They may be product updates, hot-off-the-news-wire, relevant but hard-to-find data, predictions, anecdotes, or topical items that get the audience's juices flowing.

Music can underline these important presentation points without overpowering the speaker. When professional film composers underscore dialog, they sometimes treat the spoken lines as if they were a lead melody. Using music that works well as accompaniment to a melody frequently works well with presenters' spoken lines, too. You can still use themes and melodies in a slide that will be spoken over, but take care that they don't stick out in the track's music mix, or they will compete with the message being delivered live.

**Sexy Bits.** Sexy in this context means high production value and features, such as flashy graphics, animations, videos, and even music itself. If you're scoring a still or moving visual, you will get good clues for the musical style from the visual element(s). If the featured sexy bit is your music, then go for it. This is where you can feature melody, dense or syncopated rhythms, and other musical elements that might otherwise compete with the speaker, because the speaker generally will not talk over this music feature.

**Big Closer**. This can be the same as the opening Grabber music, or might creep in over the last portion of the body of the presentation, and build to a climax at the end. The theme and style should be the same as for the Grabber.

The rest is up to your own creativity. No two composers would, or should, agree on what's the "right" music to score a soundtrack. Individual idiosyncrasies and musical personalities of composers differentiate them from each other, and vive la différence!

## FINDING PRESENTATION WORK

A corporate AV department is a good place to look for composing work. You can research Fortune 500 and other large companies in your area, make cold calls to their AV departments, and ask if you can meet with them to discuss how you may be of assistance in their music needs. You could wind up with some contract work or even a permanent job as in-house music supervisor/composer. In any case, your knowledge of presentation programs and corporate AV processes will stand you in good stead.

## TEMPING A PROJECT

"Temping a project" means placing temporary music in the project, so you and your production team can audition how each cue works. You can use library music, commercial songs, soundtracks, or your own music for various cues. The object is to determine if the styles, tempos, and impacts of the music cues work well with the images and text. After your temp music has been approved, you will replace the temporary music with your own original cues, which will have similar styles and impacts.

The following exercise will give you experience in temping a presentation.

## EXERCISE 5.2. TEMP SCORE A PRESENTATION

Temp the PowerPoint presentation **PP_DCMS.ppt** on the included CD in the **05_Presentations** folder. Use your own music files and any other music to which you have access.

You'll have to make decisions about:

1. which slides should have music
2. which piece of music you want to use for (each) slide(s)
3. when you want each music cue to start and finish
4. whether you want music files triggered for a whole slide(s) or for particular events within a slide, such as text or graphics appearing when the presenter clicks the mouse (or hits a key)

Run the PowerPoint presentation with and without music. Does the music help or hinder the presentation?

Try changing the music cues and rerun the presentation. Is it better or worse? Why?

This temping exercise is very practical. It's the same process you will go through when you work on a commercial project, and it's a very good way to make a demo for a potential employer. Offer to temp one of the company's PowerPoint presentations on a no-obligation basis. If they like your work and think it improves their presentation, they will be more likely to give you some work when the opportunity arises.

## WHAT'S NEXT?

Composing music for presentations provides a good foundation for working with interactive media. But it only gives us a glimpse of the world in which individual users control all aspects of the interactive experience. That's the exciting world we're about to enter next—the Web.

CHAPTER **6**

# WEB MUSIC

In the early days of the Internet, millions of digital music files were exchanged, taken from commercial music CDs, while most still images and movies were still in analog formats. Even so, the use of Web page soundtracks has been limited by low-speed dial-up connections. High-speed connections using cable and DSL modems are overcoming the speed limitation and opening up excellent opportunities for Web composers.

## THE WEB AND THE INTERNET

The Internet is a complex network that connects computers and other digital devices using a suite of protocols that are optimized for different types of communications, known as services. You can think of the Internet as a many-level department store, with each level specializing in a particular service. The levels include e-mail, FTP (file transfer protocol), news groups, chat, the World Wide Web, and so on. The Web is one of many services on the Internet.

The first two Internet levels created were the transport control protocol (TCP) and Internet protocol (IP). Together they form the familiar TCP/IP, the address and communications structure that enables computers to easily interconnect with hubs, switches, routers, and other computers. In 1983, after many years of gestation, the Internet was officially defined as a group of networks that use the TCP/IP protocols.

Ten years and many protocol levels later, in 1993, the Web was made available as an Internet level called hypertext protocol (HTTP). HTTP revolutionized the use of the Internet because this protocol is optimized for sharing pictures, audio, video, and other rich media, opening the door for efficient transfer of music and video files. The Web's HTTP is simple and elegant. It consists of:

- Web pages: screens of information composed in hypertext markup language (HTML)

- URLs: universal resource locators (addresses) that uniquely identify every Web page

- Hyperlinks: interactive text or graphical areas that trigger actions when a cursor hovers over or clicks on them

- Browsers: computer programs that interpret Web pages and display the results as screens

Many browsers are available for computer and mobile platforms. Internet Explorer (or just Explorer) is the most popular, used by about three-quarters of all netizens, because it's bundled free with the Windows operating systems. Netscape was the first consumer browser and is still popular. Safari ships free with Mac OS; Opera ships with Macromedia products; Lynx works on Linux OS; Sensus is for the sight-impaired and has a built-in speech reader/synthesizer; and ChiBrow is one of many children's browsers that shields inappropriate Web content from young eyes. Mozilla is the underlying technology of many browsers including Netscape, Explorer, AOL, and Firefox.

Most browsers display other useful protocols in addition to HTML, such as JavaScript, PHP, and XML. In addition, helper applications and plugins, such as QuickTime, Flash, Windows Media Player, Shockwave, and PDF (Portable Document Format) extend the versatility of browsers. The media that helper apps interpret are not technically part of the Web because they require separate, non-Web servers to store and send the media files. All browsers have common basic functions, but each browser has unique features and displays some Web pages differently than others. Since Internet Explorer is the category leader, developers try to make their applications operate properly at least in that browser.

This may seem like a bunch of techno-babble, particularly if you're a composer who isn't familiar with the Internet. Actually, it's a simplification. Keep in mind that Web and Internet technologies do have a significant impact on the way music is composed for online content. Each protocol has its strengths and limitations for communicating music and video. There are dozens of Web sites that have excellent free tutorials on all aspects of the Internet and the Web.

## MUSIC IN WEB SITES

The use of Web page soundtracks was originally limited by the slow transfer speed of dial-up Internet connections. That limitation is vanishing as users flock to high-speed Internet services, usually defined as having at least one megabit/second download speed. It's estimated that by 2010, a majority of Internet users around the world will have high-speed connections. In North America, this is already the case. Consequently, business, government, and personal Web sites are focusing on Web page music to maximize the impact of their messages and user experiences. The opportunity for Web composers is expected to grow significantly over the next decades as older Web sites add music and new Web sites design for it.

# SPECIAL CONSIDERATIONS FOR WEB SITE MUSIC

Web site music can only be triggered when an HTML event takes place, such as when:

- a Web page is loaded into a browser

- the user clicks on a page link

- the user's cursor hovers over an active region of the screen

Loops are as important for Web music as for any other interactive media. The test for whether you should use a loop or not is simply: Can I predict how long the music will play, once it starts?

If the answer is no, you should use a looped sequence for the music.

If the answer is yes, you may still want to use loops within your sequence, but the finished product likely will be better if you craft it to be the exact length that's needed and add variations to the internal loops so that the music has more interest and cadence (emotional flow).

Here's an example. The splash page for my Web site, at www. paulhoffert.ca, uses a fixed-length music cue, because I know the length of the video that plays when the page is opened. After the video is finished, my home page, www.paulhoffert.ca/home.htm, automatically opens. Since I don't know how long it will be until each user decides which link to click, I used a music loop with some variations and short melodic fragments.

The first twelve seconds is just a loop, in an attention-getting 3/8 meter. If you link out within this time period, you'll feel that the music is a short bridge to the next page. After that, the melodic fragments begin. Because they are short, you can link out before the music is finished without feeling that you've missed an important part of the melody. I experimented at first with repeating the end loop ad infinitum until a user linked out, but found that the music became annoying after a while. So I programmed a fadeout of the closing loop after about forty-five seconds.

This simple example illustrates the types of decisions that every composer has to make for every Web cue. There is no right or wrong decision, except failing to take into account as many factors as possible about how users may interact with and experience the music.

## ORCHESTRATION

There are some special considerations that are required for each type of medium, and orchestration is perhaps the greatest of these. If you watch *Star Trek* in a movie theater or home entertainment center environment, you'll note that the scenes on the Enterprise spaceship bridge usually have a very low frequency rumble, presumably the sound of the dilithium crystal drive. This sound is mainly coming from subwoofers. Watch it on a computer, and you'll likely hear none of this sound. The built-in computer speaker can't reproduce it, and even add-on computer speakers don't have the power to play very low frequency sounds. The same holds true for the low basses, tubas, and tymps that frequently are used in the music soundtrack when the bad guys appear.

So, if *Star Trek* hadn't been cancelled, and continued to run long enough that webisodes were created specifically for computers, I would expect that the program's producers and composers would re-orchestrate the sound effects and music so that these elements could be heard. One orchestration trick is to double low frequency parts an octave higher—basses with cellos, tubas with trombones, and so on. This reinforces the low frequency sounds when a listener has a full-frequency sound system and lets a listener hear the higher-octave orchestration on reduced-frequency systems.

On the other hand, even inexpensive add-on computer speakers have pretty good high-frequency response. These require low power levels, so there's usually no need to worry about flutes and such, although piccolos and high-frequency cymbals should be avoided or doubled with lower-frequency instruments.

Another orchestration consideration is dynamic range. Sound systems on computers usually don't have as great a dynamic range as do home theater systems or cinemas. One of the reasons that Web music tends to use lots of rhythm loops is that rhythm loops generally have limited dynamic range, so that you can play them softly or loudly without losing their musical intent. Music with a much larger dynamic range, such as classical music or orchestral film scores, doesn't work very well on small-dynamic-range systems. If you reduce the loudest parts so that they don't distort the system, the softest parts vanish altogether. Consequently, music with a compressed dynamic range is often more appropriate for Web applications than is music with full dynamic range.

# WEB MEDIA PLAYERS

Browser manufacturers have adopted an expedient and cost-effective strategy for playing music and other rich media through their applications. Instead of building music- and video-playing capabilities into each browser, they use a standard procedure for accessing third-party media players that play back audio and video. These are called helper applications and plug-ins. Helpers usually open external windows when they are needed, while plug-in windows are more integrated into the browser. The major AV players are Flash, Shockwave, QuickTime, Windows Media, and Real. They are commonly used for delivering music and video to Web page visitors. These players can be downloaded from their manufacturers' Web sites.

## MIDI THROUGH BROWSERS

When dial-up connections were dominant and network bandwidth was very low, MIDI files were quite popular on the Web. The most popular browser plug-ins and helpers for media were MIDI players rather than ones in use today. Some of the limitations of MIDI music files, when used with browser playback, are:

- Lack of predictable sounds on playback, even when General MIDI sounds are specified.

- Limitation of instrument sounds to the General MIDI specification of 128 instruments plus effect sounds. These exclude many instruments that soundtrack composers routinely use.

- Lack of compatibility and lack of single standard. General MIDI 1, General MIDI 2, and General MIDI Lite standards are all commonly used, but are not compatible, particularly with respect to polyphony. So a General MIDI Lite player won't play all the notes in a General MIDI 2 file.

- Mixes are not predictable because different MIDI libraries have different volumes for the same General MIDI instrument.

As we'll see in the chapter on mobile media, these limitations are worth living with if the bandwidth is very low. For the Web, however, the tipping point came when high-speed networks began to grow in popularity at the turn of the twenty-first century, when high compression MP3 and AAC codes were able to capture decent-quality music at small enough sizes to be viable using Web distribution. Since then, MIDI has greatly declined in online use.

## TECHNICAL ISSUES

A frequently asked question is "How long can a Web music file be?" There is no simple answer because many factors have to be taken into account, including the speed of the server, network, and user connection; the storage capacities of the server and of the user's computer; the fidelity (compression) that's tolerable; and so on. These and other technical issues are dealt with for all interactive media in the appendix.

# WEB MUSIC CATEGORIES

## ADVERTISEMENTS

Web advertisers have almost no cost for distributing their videos to any size audience. There is no need to buy time slots from television networks' advertising inventory. And, unlike television, the Web can deliver information about the viewers who watch the videos. The result has been a dramatic and continuing increase in Web advertising and the use of videos for that purpose. In addition, Web ads are not constrained by television's advertising length formats—generally fifteen or thirty seconds. A Web ad can be six seconds long if the producer wants a quick impact without wearing out the visitor's welcome, or it can be six minutes long if the subject and treatment warrant it. Web ads can also be linked interactively with other Web page elements, so that a user may watch six seconds or six minutes of a video.

Web videos are common in online advertising, and they often include music. Some video ads are similar to their television counterparts, but the Web also spawns thousands of video ads each year that are produced expressly for online viewing. In many cases, the products and services advertised are aimed at narrow markets that are not easily targeted by television programs. In other cases, the ads don't warrant the high costs of purchasing television time slots. In addition, production costs for Web ads are much lower than for television ads because of the lower audio and video resolution that's tolerated online.

Composers for interactive Web videos need to be able to tell interactive stories, use loop and transition techniques, create musical identities, and understand the functions of music. Many of the techniques described for temping and creating dramatic arcs in presentation programs are also applicable to interactive ad videos.

## Photography Show Ad

The enclosed CD contains a video for a Brenda Hoffert photography show, **PhotoShowAd.mov**, in folder **06_Web**. The URL that streams the ad video (www.brendahoffert.com) was included in e-mail messages to prospective attendees of the photo show at the Spoke Club in Toronto. The online ad continues to attract customers to the photographer.

Since the photographs are fine art, creative director David Tessler and Flash animator Hinna Ahmed designed a simple and elegant video. I did likewise for the music, with an orchestration that includes some sparse acoustic strings and flute. I used a small ensemble for intimacy and to draw the listener into the visual experience.

...........................................................................................

## EXERCISE 6.1. SCORE A WEB AD

1. Load the **PhotoShowAd.mov** on the enclosed CD in the folder **06_Web** into your sequencer, and set it up so you can sync with the video but not hear the original music track.
2. Watch the video several times through until you get a sense of its internal rhythms and cadence (emotional ups and downs).
3. Compose original music for the video, taking into account that it will be played on computers with limited sound playback capabilities.

4. Compare your soundtrack with the original. Did you take a different approach? Did you decide to "hit" some of the animation actions instead of "playing through" them, as the original does? Notice how the internal rhythms of the video combine with the rhythms in your music.

5. Save your music as **WebAd.wav** in the **Advertisements** subfolder of your **DemoMusic** folder.

## Auto Ads

Automobiles are just one example of the many types of retail merchandise that are promoted and sold online using music-laden videos. The videos provide both information and entertainment for those interested in new and used cars.

Note: This and other URLs cited were operational when this book was published. In the event that some of the videos or Web sites may be taken offline in the future, please visit this book's companion Web site, www.interactivemusicbook.com, for up-to-date links and to search the Web for similar examples.

### Autobytel Web Site

This Web site contains dozens of ad videos for cars, car accessories, and other related merchandise. Sites like this one are in continual need of composers and music for inexpensive ad and promo videos that change with model years and seasons.

www.autobytel.com

## PRESENTATIONS, MINI-DRAMAS, SITCOMS, ETC.

Media guru Marshall McLuhan noted that when a new technology is introduced, its first uses echo the uses of older media, because that's what people are familiar with. The Web is no exception. Web slideshows, mini-dramas, and episodic (webisodic) dramas, comedies, and soaps are all available online. The same dramatic and functional techniques discussed in earlier chapters apply to these content types on the Web.

### EXERCISE 6.2. SCORE A WEBISODE

1. Load the file **DetectiveOne.mov**, on the enclosed CD in the folder **06_Web**, into your sequencer, and set it up so you can sync with the video but not hear the original music track.
2. Watch the video several times through until you get a sense of its internal rhythms and cadence (emotional ups and downs).
3. Compose original music for the video, taking care to change the mood, tempo, and orchestration, if you think the visual story warrants it.
4. Try matching the tempo of your music to some of the tempos inherent in the video, such as the tempo of the running feet hitting the ground.
5. Compare your soundtrack with the original. Did you take a different approach?
6. Save your music as **DetectiveOne.wav** in the **Webisode** subfolder in your **DemoMusic** folder.

## ANIMATIONS

Many of the videos on the Web are animations. The popularity of Web animations is partly due to the acceptance by netizens of low-production-value animation, usually done in Flash, which is much less expensive to produce than live-action videos. These range from two- or three-cell loops to full-motion graphics, simulations, and cartoons. They may be informational, entertaining, educational, or a combination of these.

Music soundtracks for animation tend to use hard synchronization of screen events with musical events, "punching up" the
story line with musical "hits." This type of music treatment was
honed in the early days of Hollywood cartoons, which is why it's
still known as Mickey Mousing the picture.

Composers frequently first build "click tracks" (or "clicks")—
tempo and meter structures that audibly click a metronome
beat. These are also called tempo maps. They are fine-tuned until
the picture actions match up with music beats. Once the click
matches the action, the music is filled in; it's a "paint-by-numbers"
approach. Every animation requires its own approach, however,
since the types of animations range from a beating heart for an
anatomy lesson to a dramatic movie-like narrative.

## EXERCISE 6.3. SCORE ANOTHER WEBISODE

Play the video **WeedsEugene.mov** on the included CD. This
comic animation uses music that plays against the story. The
VO (voiceover) copy has lines such as "shrill, irritated voice,"
"nightmares," and "wetting the bed," but the music just keeps its
pleasant-sounding guitar groove throughout. Does the music
play as ironic comedy for you, or would a soundtrack that uses a
dramatic arc work better? The soundtracks for other webisodes
in this "Weeds" series vary in their styles and creative approaches.
Check them out at:

www.zed.cbc.ca/go?~main~command=next&~main~FILTER
_KEY=159157&c=searchResults&FILTER_KEY=159157

1. Compose your own soundtrack for **WeedsEugene.mov**.
   Save it in your **DemoMusic** Folder.
2. Play your soundtrack and the original for some friends
   and ask for their comments. It's not so important which
   music they like better—only whether the webisode makes
   its point better with one or the other.

## HOME PAGE IDENTITIES

The use of musical identities, logos, and themes on Web site home
pages can be accompanied by video or animation. Using music for
a text-dominated Web page is similar to using music in a Power-

Point presentation and can effectively enrich and add dimension to the user experience. Remember to research the property, identify the personality of the product or company, and let the music tell the story.

## EXERCISE 6.4. GLENN GOULD FOUNDATION HOME PAGE

1. Go to the home page of the Glenn Gould Foundation, www.glenngould.ca/.
2. Surf the site to get a sense of the information and identity that the Glenn Gould Foundation is portraying.
3. Create a soundtrack for this homepage. You can create your own music to portray the Glenn Gould Foundation, which need not relate to either the music of Bach, of which Glenn Gould was a noted interpreter, or Glenn Gould's performances.

   **Note 1:** Bach compositions are in the public domain and may be used freely.
   **Note 2:** Recordings of Bach compositions that were made in the past fifty years may not be used commercially without permission of the record company that owns the sound recordings, although you can use such recordings for educational purposes, such as for completing this exercise.

4. Save your music file as **GouldHomePage.wav** in your **DemoMusic** folder.

Currently, only a small percentage of home pages use music. Eventually, most will use music to identify their owners. Since there are tens of millions of home pages, the work potential for composers is enormous, even if just a small percentage of Web sites adds music each year.

## SHOPPING SITES

Ever notice that there's background music playing in almost every store you go into? The same will soon be true for most Web stores. Online shoppers will have music tailored to their individual tastes, much like sophisticated commercial sites create individually tailored Web pages for their customers based on their person-alities and buying profiles. The amount of interactivity and rich media will continue to vary from site to site.

## INFORMATION SITES

There are two basic types of informational Web sites: those that aim to objectively inform their users and those that focus on marketing products and services. The latter generally have greater resources available for creation and maintenance, and they are more likely to use interactivity and music.

## PROMOTIONAL SITES

The Web is filled with sites whose main function is to market and promote products, services, and organizations. The live-action video **GotHerbs.mov**, on your included CD in the folder **06_Web**, was shot and scored by Jonathan Feist, my editor for this book. The video is a Web promotion for restoring the Shaker Herb-Drying House, maintained by the Historical Commis-sion in Harvard, Massachusetts (www.jonathanfeist.com/Pages/HarvardPreservation.html).

## EXERCISE 6.5. MUSIC FOR SHOPPING, INFORMATION, AND PROMOTIONAL SITES

1. Compose your own score for **GotHerbs.mov**. The infor-mation is given by a VO track, which can be played in QuickTime separately from the music track, so you can mute the original music while still listening to the voice. Professional composers frequently take note of when VO phrases start and stop, and are careful to keep their possibly intrusive melodies and rhythm fills in the spaces between the voice phrases, so as not to compete with the information.
2. Find a Web site homepage that illustrates (a) shopping, (b) information, or (c) promotion—one that's likely to improve with your music.

3. Use the screen snapshot capability of your operating system, <Command-Shift-4> for Mac OS and the <PRINTSCREEN> key for Windows, to capture the image of the home page.

4. Import the home page screen snapshot into QuickTime, and save it as a QuickTime movie. Note: You can have a movie with just a single frame.

5. Import the QuickTime file into your music sequencer as a video/movie. Then compose music that helps express an underlying or explicit message in the home page.

## OPTIONAL ADVANCED EXERCISE

6. Use a screen motion-capture program such as Snapz Pro for Mac OS or Camtasia for Windows to capture a video file of your session on the selected Web sites.

7. Import this video into your sequencer, and compose music that is synchronized with the activities that you've captured.

## BROWSER GAMES

Web games are probably the most popular content category online. There are thousands of Web sites offering games, many with more than one hundred games on a single site.

The major difference between games delivered within Web sites and games played from a DVD in a computer is that browser games are restricted in features and visual rendering. Browser games usually use much smaller files, less photo-realistic animation, and so on. On the other hand, browser games have one great advantage over all other platforms: they are available to everyone with a computer, and are inter-operable (work on all computer platforms). It doesn't matter whether you are using an Apple, Dell, or clone computer or whether your operating system is Windows XP, Linux, or Mac OS X. If a Web game works within Internet Explorer on one platform, it likely will do so on the others.

Most Web games are implemented in Flash. Since users already have the helper application, there's no need to download a special gaming engine and player.

Web games are very popular on sites aimed at young children, in part because the simple graphics and excellent animation capabilities of Flash are appealing to kids. An example of a site aimed at youth, particularly young girls, is NeoPets, www.neopets.com/gameroom.phtml. It has hundreds of games categorized as puzzles, action, and luck/chance. Each has a unique music soundtrack, and the games cover a broad spectrum of musical styles, from ambient to rhythmic. Many of these soundtracks are excellent examples of well-planned and -executed Web music, particularly the use of loops.

Music for games will be discussed thoroughly in the Game Music chapters.

## HTML WEB AUTHORING

Although browser helper and plug-in AV players are free, the corresponding Web authoring applications for audio and video generally have to be purchased. Simple authoring systems, such as QuickTime Pro, are relatively inexpensive, while more complex and powerful systems, such as Flash or Director, are more costly and more capable.

When an audio or video file is referenced in an HTML document, its suffix (such as .mp3, .wav, .mid, .mov, etc.) is read by the user's browser. If a helper or plug-in application for that file type exists on the user's computer, the helper or plug-in is loaded, and the file is played. Usually, the file will be located on the Web server, from which it needs to be downloaded before it can be played. Some players and file types can be streamed, provided they have been prepared and saved as streaming files. In these cases, there is much less delay before the file can be played.

Although you don't have to be an HTML programmer to be an interactive composer, it certainly is an asset to understand how music is delivered, synchronized (or not), processed, and played through a browser interface. The basic concepts of HTML, Flash, and game programming are similar, so that knowledge of HTML will assist you in understanding the others, as well.

HTML authoring applications are available for all computer platforms at price points ranging from free to shareware to professional applications such as Macromedia Dreamweaver. Internet resources for learning HTML and downloading HTML editors are available for free on the Internet.

You also can use Microsoft Word or other word processors to edit and compose HTML documents, since they are composed only of text. The advantage of dedicated HTML editors is that they automate the code-writing process, check for errors, allow you to preview both the code and the displayed page in the browser at the same time, and generally handle the most time-consuming and ugliest parts of the coding. This lets you concentrate on designing the Web pages rather than coding them.

The details of HTML programming are beyond the scope of this book, but the following exercise will help you demo your music using real Web pages. It contains HTML code that will play music from Web pages in various scenarios. All you have to do is change the names of the music files (in bold type) to the names of your own music files, keep your music files in the same folder as the HTML page, and add the HTML coding (in the Courier font) to the source code of the Web page that you're working on. You can get the source code of the Web page by Right-clicking (Windows) or Control-clicking (Mac) on the page and choosing the "Save Source Code to Disk" option.

Bear in mind that HTML programming, while straightforward and simple in its language and syntax, is made more complicated because different browsers and different versions of the same browser interpret HTML differently. Experienced HTML programmers should be consulted before you place any HTML pages that you've coded on the Web. It might work on your computer's browser, but don't assume it will work on others.

### HTML Code for EMBED Command

The HTML command most often used to embed audio objects in Web pages is the EMBED command. This is the command used to play sound and video objects. By default, it will display a graphical controller, allowing the user to pause or replay the audio file, but the controls may be removed using optional parameter commands. Though EMBED is not an officially supported HTML command, most browsers understand it, and developers use it regularly. All the parameter commands are not universal to all browsers, but the basics are relatively safe to use.

**Fig. 6.1.** Embed Controller

SRC—The URL of the sound file. It will play files of any type for which the user's browser has a plug-in, but commonly AIFF, WAV, MIDI, MOV.

HEIGHT—Numeric value in pixels. The height of the controller, in pixels. The minimum value here is 2, but since the controller is 16 pixels high, 16 is a common value. For embedded video objects, the number needs to be large enough for the video window.

WIDTH—Numeric value in pixels. The length of the controller (or video window), in pixels.

AUTOSTART—True/False. By default, it is set to "true," which automatically plays the file as soon as the page is loaded. "False" requires the user to initiate playback with an interaction.

CONTROLLER—True/False. Indicates whether or not the controller is displayed on the screen.

HIDDEN—(No value needed.) Hides the controller.

LOOP TRUE/FALSE—Indicates whether the file plays once or loops continuously. By default, it is set to "false."

VOLUME—Number between 0 (off) and 100 (full). This volume controller is in relation to the user's current system and hardware settings. The default is 50.

## EXERCISE 6.6. HTML FOR PLAYING MUSIC IN WEB PAGES

1. Open your browser. From the File menu, select Open File and navigate to the folder **06_Web** on your included CD.
2. Open the file **htmlMusic.htm**. It will open in a window of your browser and start playing a music file from the CD. The music file being played is named **PageMusic1.wav**.
3. The Web page is a self-annotated primer on writing HTML code for playing music in Web pages. There are examples for using music in four different ways, automatically when a page is opened and under user control. The examples include MP3, WAV, and MIDI files.

4. Here's the code in the **htmlMusic.htm** file to play a WAV file.

```
<EMBED SRC="PageMusic1.wav"
WIDTH="146" HEIGHT="16" VOLUME="100"
AUTOSTART="true" CONTROLLER="true"
CONTROLS="SMALLCONSOLE"

<NOEMBED><BGSOUND SRC="PageMusic1.wav"
/></NOEMBED></EMBED>
```

**Note 1.** The extra code beginning with "<NOEMBED>" is necessary for maximum compatibility with older versions of Internet Explorer. This means you must enter your music filename in two places.
**Note 2.** The Autostart parameter is set to "true."

5. Here's the HTML code to play an MP3 file **PageMusic2. mp3** under user control.

```
<EMBED SRC="PageMusic2.mp3"
WIDTH="146" HEIGHT="16" VOLUME="100"
AUTOSTART="false" CONTROLLER="true"
CONTROLS="SMALLCONSOLE"

<NOEMBED><BGSOUND SRC="PageMusic2.mp3"
LOOP=1></NOEMBED></EMBED></P>
```

**Note 1.** The AUTOSTART parameter is set to "false," allowing the user to control the playing of the file.
**Note 2.** The type of music file (MP3, WAV, MIDI, etc.) doesn't affect the HTML code, but it will play only if the helper application, such as QuickTime or Windows Media Player, can play that file type.

6. Here's the HTML code to play a music file **pagemusic3. wav** by clicking a button.

```
<P CLASS="style1"><B>Click button to
play pagemusic3.wav</B><BR>

 <P CLASS="style1"><A HREF="pagemusic3.
wav"><IMG SRC="button.jpg" BORDER="3"></
A> </P>
```

**Note 1.** You need a graphic image file of a button named **button.jpg** for this to work.

7. Here's the HTML code to play a MIDI music file named **PageMusic4.mid** from a link.

```
<P CLASS="style1"><A HREF="PageMusic4.
mid"> Click here to play <span class=
"style4">PageMusic4.mid</span> </A> </P>
```

**Note 1.** A helper application, such as QuickTime or Windows Media Player, plays the music file, provided the file type is playable by the helper.
**Note 2.** The music file is assumed to be in the same disk folder as the HTML page file.

## EXERCISE 6.7. ADD MUSIC TO A WEB PAGE

1. Find a simple Web page that you'd like to add music to—one without frames (separate rectangular areas)—and copy its source code (see earlier) into **WebPage**, a new subfolder that you create inside the folder **DemoMusic**.
2. Compose your music for the Web page, and save it in your new **WebPage** subfolder.
3. Open the **htmlMusic.htm** Web page in an HTML editor or word processor.
4. Open the Web page that you want to add music to in the same editor or word processor. The file is in your **DemoMusic** folder, in the **WebPage** subfolder.
5. Copy the relevant HTML code from the **htmlMusic.htm** document into the Web page you're adding music to.
6. Change the name of the music file from **PageMusicx.xxx** to the name of your music file. Save the document.
7. In your browser, under the File menu, select Open File and then select the new Web page that you modified. It will have your music in it.

## FLASH

The most popular authoring system for Web pages with music, animation, and video is Macromedia Flash. Like Microsoft's PowerPoint, Flash is a dominant program in its category. The

Flash player is on almost every computer that accesses the Web and is used by more than one million Web programmers. If you visit a Web site that has lots of animation and sync sound, there's a good chance that it's been programmed with Flash.

That's why it's a good idea for Web composers to be familiar with Flash. You don't have to be a Flash programmer, but you should at least be conversant with Flash's capabilities, which are ideal for interactive music. Flash's audio commands allow you to:

- repeat a music file a fixed number of times or indefinitely (looped)

- trigger a musical change when a screen event occurs (cursor, etc.)

- set the volume at any point in the music

- program crescendos and decrescendos

- set the pan (left/right) at any point in the music

- mix (layer) several music and audio track(s)

- use random choices for audio files or parameters, making each experience of the same Web page different

Flash lets you play continuously, and also allows you to synchronize a soundtrack to video or animation. You can add sounds to Web page buttons, and you can make sound fade in and out.

There are two types of audio in Flash: event sounds and stream sounds. An event sound must be downloaded completely to the user's appliance before it begins playing. Stream sounds begin playing as soon as the first few frames have been downloaded and are synchronized to the Flash Timeline, a measurement in minutes, seconds, and frames that runs from the beginning to the end of a Flash file.

Musical events can be started at specific times (specified in frame numbers or seconds) or triggered by interactive events such as mouse clicks, key presses, download completions, and so on. Flash's ability to mix audio tracks and do fade-ins and fade-outs enables true crossfades between outgoing and incoming music tracks. That means a composer can decide that a music file should finish playing a beat, measure, or phrase before ending or triggering the playing of a new music file or other process. This allows for much more natural and professional transitions than HTML authoring.

You can use shared library sounds to link in many different documents, and you can trigger any video or audio event based on the completion of a sound. Flash also allows you to add user playback controls onscreen such as Stop, Pause, and Rewind.

## EXAMPLE: USER CONTROLS OF FLASH FILES

A good example of how Flash can layer soundtracks that are user controllable is the "Nothing and Nowhere" Web site, which is at www.nothingandnowhere.com/flash4.html. Clicking on the speaker icon at the bottom right of the screen brings up a menu of sound controls that allow the user, in real time, to modify the volume of the background music, the sound effects, and the music clips. Changing the onscreen controls changes the mix as you listen to it, allowing each user to customize the experience.

## FORMATS FOR FLASH AUTHORING

When you're delivering music files to a Flash programmer, you should use a high fidelity uncompressed audio format such as WAV or AIFF, not MP3 or AAC. The Flash programmer will then mix the music and other audio files into a single sound file and compress it appropriately for the particular intended use. In some cases, Web site audio/visual files are made available in several quality and compression levels so users can choose the best fit for their equipment and Internet connection.

## EXERCISE 6.8. ADD FLASH MUSIC TO A WEB PAGE

This exercise requires the Flash authoring application, not just the Flash player. Skip this exercise if you don't have access to the Flash authoring application. If you're using Mac OS, replace the Control key with the Command key.

1. Launch Flash and select **File** > New (Control-N) from the menu bar.
2. Select **File** > Import > Import to Stage (Control-R) to import the music file **PageMusic1.wav** from the included audio file.

3. All content used in Flash is stored in the Library Panel. If it's not yet visible on your screen, select **Window** > Library (Control-L) from the menu bar.

4. To add the music file to your document, click and drag the music file from the Library Panel onto the stage.

5. Notice that the first frame of the working Layer in the Timeline is no longer empty. It contains a visual reference to the music file in the shape of a waveform.

6. Click the Frame with the waveform to select it in the Timeline.

7. The Property Inspector Panel (Control-F3) has a Synch field. Note that the music file is now set to "STREAM." Flash makes it easy to stream audio, which doesn't need to be downloaded to the user's device before playing.

8. Extend the Timeline so that the total number of Frames in the file is equal to the duration of the music file. Select **Insert** > Timeline > Frame (F5 from the menu bar) and add frames (F5 key is easiest) until you see the end of the waveform in the selected Layer.

9. The FLA source file is completed. This must be published as a SWF file, in order for it to work with a Flash player in the user's device.

10. Select **File** > Publish Settings (Control-Shift-F12) from the Menu Bar. The Publish Settings Dialog Box will open.

11. Choose the Formats tab and check the Flash (.swf) and HTML (.html) checkboxes, and then click OK.

12. Select **File** > Publish (Shift-F12) to export the .swf and .html files to your **DemoMusic** folder.

13. Flash will automatically generate the HTML Object > EMBED tags and parameters required to display and play the Flash file in a browser.

14. Sample music files are named **streamingaudio.fla** (the Flash source file), **streamingaudio.swf** (Shockwave file for the Flash Player application), and **streamingaudio. html** (an HTML coded Web page that uses Flash to stream a file named **streamingaudio.swf**; see the sidebar, following).

### Stream a Music File [streamingaudio.swf] Using Flash

Here's the HTML code for triggering a music file built using Flash:

```
<!--URL'S USED IN THE MOVIE-->

<!--TEXT USED IN THE MOVIE-->

<OBJECT CLASSID="CLSID:D27CDB6E-AE6D-
11CF-96B8-444553540000" CODEBASE=
"HTTP://FPDOWNLOAD.MACROMEDIA.COM/
PUB/SHOCKWAVE/CABS/FLASH/SWFLASH.
CAB#VERSION=7,0,0,0" WIDTH="100"
HEIGHT="100" ID="STREAMING AUDIO"
ALIGN="MIDDLE">

<PARAM NAME="ALLOWSCRIPTACCESS"
VALUE="SAMEDOMAIN" />

<PARAM NAME="MOVIE"
VALUE="STREAMINGAUDIO.SWF" />

<PARAM NAME="QUALITY" VALUE="HIGH" />

<PARAM NAME="BGCOLOR" VALUE="#FFFFFF" />

<EMBED SRC="STREAMING AUDIO.SWF"
QUALITY="HIGH" BGCOLOR="#FFFFFF"
WIDTH="100" HEIGHT="100" NAME="STREAMING
AUDIO" ALIGN="MIDDLE" ALLOWSCRIPTACC
ESS="SAMEDOMAIN" TYPE="APPLICATION/X-
SHOCKWAVE-FLASH" PLUGINSPAGE="HTTP://WWW.
MACROMEDIA.COM/GO/GETFLASHPLAYER" />

</OBJECT>
```

# TO TECH OR NOT TO TECH, THAT'S THE QUESTION

It's not necessary to learn HTML or Flash programming to be a successful Web site composer, but it doesn't hurt. As a serious composer, you should get to know the basic lingo and understand how far you can push programmers to realize your musical ideas. It's a bit like knowing how to use your music sequencer program. You can create great music without knowing how to use a sequencer (by hiring a technician, for example), but you won't be able to maximize your creative potential unless you know at least what your sequencer can and cannot do.

Please refer to the appendix on Technical Info, for more information about technology issues that apply to all interactive media. The interplay between creativity and technology is central to all media soundtrack composing.

## WHAT'S NEXT?

While the Web represents a bright future of opportunities for interactive composers, the greatest commercial activity in interactive soundtracks today is for videogames. In the next chapters, we'll look at where the action is and how to address it.

CHAPTER **7**

# VIDEOGAME MUSIC

Games are the most commercially developed interactive media. Gaming consoles and software generate more income than the film business. Videogame popularity is due in part to game soundtracks, which are more widespread, featured, and sophisticated than music soundtracks in any other interactive media.

# VIDEOGAME STRUCTURE

All the principles and techniques discussed so far also apply to videogame soundtracks. But videogames have their own unique structures that require special consideration by composers. Two chapters in this book are devoted to videogames, plus sections of other chapters, because it's such a broad topic, with a great diversity of genres and subgenres. Although the musical style will vary greatly from one genre to another and from one title to the next, the types of scenes will generally fall into just a few categories. Following is a functional breakdown of these structural categories. Screenshots of each of the scene categories, from the videogame WumpasWorld, are on the included CD, in the folder **07_Game**.

## ATTRACTOR

This screen is also known as a splash. The purpose is to attract players to start the game. Sometimes the visual is static, and sometimes there's an animation or movie on a loop. The music is always looped and is usually a version of one of the main themes. The attention-getting splash remains on the player's screen until one of the play controls is activated.

Lineage is one of the more popular online games. Although ongoing game play requires payment, you can download the game engine at www.lineage.com, check out the attractor screen, and listen to the excellent orchestral music for free.

## STARTUP

Many games have startup sections that are short and noninteractive, and set the scene for the first situation and ultimate goal of the game. The visuals are frequently "canned" (premade) videos with excellent production value. Unlike game situations, whose visuals are created on the fly, according to the interactions with players, the startup screen can play a linear movie that has a clear beginning and end. The composer should treat a startup movie like scoring a film cue, and can hit (synchronize) the music with screen events because they will always occur at the same time interval from the start of the scene.

# SITUATION

The essence of a game is to present a player with situations, also known as challenges. Situations can be crises, problems, puzzles, or quests, but in almost every case, there are near-term and ultimate objectives that need to be fulfilled. Situation music will vary greatly, depending on the particular game. A video checkers game would likely require a different musical style and theme than an action shoot-'em-up game. Still, every situation requires looped music that must not become too monotonous after many repetitions, because it can take a long time to achieve the goal of a situation and move to the next musical sequence.

# TRANSITION

Transitions are short, non-interactive scenes that give players a chance to catch their breath and savor an achievement or rue a failure. Like the startup section, transitions are usually canned and can be scored like movie scenes.

# SUCCESS

Success scenes are also known as achievement, completion, or winning, and are a type of transition. They occur when a near-term or ultimate goal is accomplished. In checkers, you might get a king as a near-term goal and/or win the game as the ultimate goal. In a shoot-'em-up action game, you might kill all the bad guys within a scene for the near-term goal and/or rescue the hostages as the ultimate goal. Success music is, needless to say, upbeat and congratulatory. The video is canned.

# FAILURE

Failure scenes occur when a player loses the ability to achieve an objective. The reasons vary from game to game, but the result is always that the player must begin a fresh game, or start from the beginning of the current or previous level. The accompanying music is usually somber, but sometimes emphasizes the coming challenge in a more positive mood so as not to discourage the player. The video is canned.

## ULTIMATE FAILURE

The ending scene is the ultimate game failure, when a player no longer has the chance to achieve the ultimate objective. This can happen when the player loses to an opponent or runs out of resources, such as lives, playing pieces, or time. The video is usually canned.

## ULTIMATE SUCCESS

A game ends successfully when the ultimate goal is achieved. The music should reflect the ultimate positive termination, and may recap (repeat) an earlier main or success theme. The video is usually canned.

## CLOSING CREDITS

Unlike many other interactive media, such as presentations or mobile phone games, videogames usually have a closing credits section with credit cards or a crawl, which list the names and jobs of people who worked on the videogame. Composers love credit segments because they are long and the music can be composed to a fixed length. Like film credits, it's not unusual to link many of the themes and musical ideas that were in the body of the game, sort of like an overture but at the end. Credit music is usually good for a composer's demo disk.

## EXERCISE 7.1. TEMP A GAME

In this exercise, you will compose music for or place pre-composed music in excerpts from the videogame *Silverwing*, by NDi Media. The full game has thirteen situations (levels). The scenes and associated music cues are:

| Source Video | Temp Music (on CD) |
|---|---|
| 1_attractor.mov | 1_attractor.wav |
| 2_startup.mov | 2_startup.wav |
| 3_situation1.mov | 3_situation1.wav |
| 4_transition.mov | 4_transition.wav |

1. Load each video segment from the included CD within the folder **07_Game** in the subfolder **GameSegments**, into your music sequencer.

2. Compose music for each video scene. Mix each of your cues to a stereo file. You will end up with a separate music file for each scene: **1_attractor.mov**, **2_startup.mov**, **3_situation1.mov**, and **4_transition.mov**. Note that this game uses the same transition scene (**4_transition.mov**) for both failure and success. You may wish to compose separate music cues for success or failure, even though the scene will be the same. In this case, make a copy of the **4_transition.mov** file and name it **5_transition2.mov**. Use one file for success music and the other file for failure music.

4. Load the video **Game.mov**, also in the **GameSegments** subfolder, into your sequencer. This video is an edited assembly of the separate scenes for which you composed music.

5. Load your mixed music cues into a single sequence, aligning the beginning of each cue at a video scene change. Apply whichever transitions you would use in the real game, such as repeats and/or crossfades, to your mixed cues, so that you end up with a single stereo music file that plays from beginning to end and syncs with the **Game.mov** file.

6. You have created a videogame demo for your demo disk. Name your music track **Game.wav** and save it to a new subfolder **Games** in your **DemoMusic** folder. Save also each of the component music sequences of **Game.wav** to the same folder.

7. Add your **Game.mov** soundtrack to the **Game.mov** video in QuickTimePro, turn off the commercial soundtrack (use Command-j), turn on your new soundtrack, and save the movie in your **DemoMusic** folder. You can use this file to demonstrate your game composing.

8. Listen to your game music demo. Evaluate its successes and shortcomings, and redo any segments that you think can be improved. Compare the effect of your music to the original music soundtrack.

# VIDEOGAME PLATFORMS

Gaming is immensely popular because it offers players a very high degree of interaction. Players can continually change the course of events, whether by rolling dice, choosing which card to play, moving a virtual chess piece, or manipulating the controls on a videogame console. The earliest gaming consoles in the 1970s had only the crudest image resolution and jerky motion, yet sales grew into the multi-billions of dollars almost overnight. One reason was the use of musical sounds from the very outset that, in addition to providing entertainment, gave feedback to players about their successes, failures, and levels of play. Game soundtracks are entertaining, interactive, and functional.

Videogames have surpassed movies as vehicles of pop culture, particularly among children, teenagers, and young adults. Titles such as *Grand Theft Auto, Halo, Legend of Zelda, Myst, Doom, Madden NFL, Tony Hawk's Pro Skater, Final Fantasy, Barbie's Fashion, Super-Mario, Pac-Man,* and *The Sims* are just a few of the dozens of games that have become touchstones of our culture.

Some use the term "videogame" to include all games that use electronics, a screen, and interactive controls. Others apply the term more precisely, limited to only those games with television screens and hand controllers with buttons. In this chapter, we'll take the middle ground, including computer games that may use a mouse and keyboard for input, but excluding computer games that are delivered through a browser. Those games were discussed in the chapter on Web music. We'll also exclude portable console games, which will be discussed in the chapter on mobile media, because their form factors, screens, and playing environments have much in common with other mobile applications.

The three main videogame platforms we'll discuss are:

- arcade games

- home consoles

- computer games

## ARCADE GAMES

Arcade videogames are played in public spaces—pool halls, hotel gaming rooms, malls, and, of course, game arcades. Companies purchase them and charge users to play. Usually, the games have coin or bill slots, and require players to ante up in order to make the game functional. Sometimes, users pay a fee for a time interval of play and sometimes they pay for a game session, which is determined by achieving a threshold (the next level) or depleting a resource (balls in a pinball game, outs in a baseball game, lives in a role-playing game). The length of each game play is designed to be short, in order to maximize profit.

Arcade game hardware must be very sturdy and robust, since it is abused more than home gaming consoles. Arcade games can have many types of interactive controllers, including joysticks, trackballs, steering wheels, footboards, guns, bicycles, motorcycles, skis, oars, punching bags, soccer goalposts, and basketball nets. Many of these are too costly and cumbersome for home use.

**Fig. 7.1.** In the Groove 2 (top left), Outrun 2 (bottom left), House of the Dead (right)

Music in arcade games has many functions, one of which is to attract potential players in the vicinity of a game to plunk their money in the slot and play. Consequently, the music used for the splash (attractor) scenes must convey the essence of what a player should expect from a game—suspense, action, fun, thrills, exercise, and so on. The splash music is usually taken from one or more of the music cues in the game.

The first killer arcade game was *Pong*, in 1972. Designed by Al Alcorn, it's a simple single-player game in which the player controls the horizontal screen position of a paddle with a rotating knob. The objective is to move the paddle back and forth across the bottom of the screen to block passage of and rebound a ball. If the ball isn't successfully blocked, it falls off the bottom of the screen and the player loses a point. Even in this early game, musical sounds accompanied the blocks or misses of the ball, the advance to higher levels of play, and the ultimate loss of all points for the end of the game.

As arcade games became more sophisticated and more technically capable, game music followed suit, not only in musical complexity and fidelity, but also in the relative importance of music to the player's experience. When you walk into a game arcade, the music and sound effects are loud, with lots of bass. That's because the arcade games are large and can house big speakers and powerful audio amplifiers. In fact, someone visiting an arcade for the first time would likely rank music as the most prominent and important aspect of the games.

Composers take advantage of the full fidelity and high volume levels of arcade games. They use the low and high ends of the frequency spectrum in their orchestrations to add both power and punch, emphasizing onscreen actions, such as bomb drops and the like. Urban music that sounds thin when played through computer speakers can be thumping and thudding when played through arcade game amps and speakers, which can be optimized for each game's musical requirements. Likewise, dance music, with its required strong and powerful beats, works great in an arcade, where the sound levels and frequency response are suitable for drowning out the sound of feet jumping up and down on dance-game sensors.

The attractor music for arcade games is perhaps more important than for other gaming types, because it must entice the potential player to approach the game to check out the attractor screens, which work with the music to pry coins, bills, and credit cards from players' pockets. In contrast, most other videogames have already been purchased before the player gets to see the first screen and hear the first music.

## EXERCISE 7.2. ARCADE GAMES

1. Start a Games section in your notebook for observing and analyzing how music is used in games. The first subsection will be for arcade games.
   a. Go to a video arcade and watch gamers playing at least five different arcade games.
   b. Make notes about how music is used in:

   - the splash screen
   - the startup screen
   - different levels and modes of play
   - transitions between modes or levels of play
   - achieving an objective, such as moving to the next level, defeating an enemy, or solving a puzzle

   c. Play the games yourself. Note how you react to the music, paying particular attention to the emotional impact of the music and the functions it serves, such as indicating which mode and level of play you're in.

## HOME GAMING CONSOLES

A videogame console is a hardware device that contains the "brains" for a game but not the monitor or speakers that a player needs to watch and listen to.

The greatest cost for a good gaming platform is the screen display, so in order to keep the price low, manufacturers of home videogame consoles do not include a screen. Instead, they provide a video and audio output that connects to any television set, which provides both the screen and the sound (amplifier and speakers). This makes home consoles affordable but tethers the players to wherever the television set is located.

The fortunes of game consoles ride almost entirely on the available game titles. The Atari VCS was a commercial flop for its first three years on the market until Atari bought the rights to the successful arcade game *Space Invaders*, and ported it to the VCS platform. Riding on the consumer appeal of the *Space Invaders* application, Atari went on to sell twenty-five thousand VCS consoles and made $100 million. It was the first successful home-gaming venture.

**Fig. 7.2.** Atari VCS Home Gaming Console (1977), *Space Invaders*

In the early days of video gaming, homes usually had only a single color television, and it was usually located in the living room. Thus, home gamers would disrupt the leisure activities of other family members by preventing them from watching television while they were playing. Today, many families have more than one television set, and some have separate activity/ entertainment rooms where gaming takes place, so there is less disruption.

In addition, young adults, who are a significant segment of the home videogame market, frequently live away from their families, in university dorms or apartments where television set contention is less severe. Still, home gaming continues to cause problems for many players, particularly when the sound of repeated music loops escapes from the play area and intrudes on the concentration of others who cohabit.

Console games have some features that easily trump arcade games. The most obvious is the wide range of titles available in CD, mini-CD, DVD, or cartridge formats. This is obviously more appealing to players than having just a single-title game in an arcade device. In order to accommodate different types of games, console game platforms need very powerful microprocessors and co-processors, rivaling or exceeding the capabilities of those in home computers. Social gaming is encouraged by multiple hand-controller inputs in consoles that allow up to four gamers to play simultaneously.

And home consoles are transportable. You can pack a console game and its accessories into a reasonable-sized box to take on a vacation or to a friend's house. You can also pack up your gaming gear and put it away in a closet, freeing the space in your home for other uses.

Home-gaming consoles can play CDs and DVDs with high quality digital music, sound effects, and speech. This gives composers much more flexibility in creating music soundtracks. Still, home consoles use the often low-quality sound playback built into the connected television set. But as television audio has increased in quality, so has the playback quality of console games. When you play a console game on a surround-sound woofer-equipped home theater system, the audio fidelity surpasses what you might hear from an arcade game.

## DIFFERENCES FOR COMPOSERS

Some of the differences between arcade and console platforms require creative adjustments from composers. The attractor screens for arcade games are usually rhythmic, loud, and unrelenting, in order to attract potential gaming customers from across the aisle. Home console attractor-screen music, on the other hand, can have greater dynamic and emotional range and can be less strident. The function of the console-game splash screen is simply to get the players in the mood for the game's subject and psychological environment, while they get their hand controllers ready and sit down to play.

Another general difference between arcade and console game music is in the length of cues and loops. Arcade game scenes tend to be shorter, so that players will drop more coins or card credits into the slot. This means that music cues and loops tend to be shorter as well. Home console videogame scenes, on the other hand, are played over longer periods of time, allowing for longer loops, themes, and cues.

In 2000, the first videogame consoles with Internet connections became available, and they ushered in a new era of multiplayer networked gaming. Videogame consoles with Internet connections allow for the downloading of games, add-on scenes, cheats (time-saving code patches), music, and other digital data from the network server to a player's console or between two players' consoles. Home gamers can now interact with other players who aren't physically in the same room. They can play games with neighbors down the block or halfway around the world, transcending the limitations of place. In 2004, 15 percent of gaming was networked, and forecasts of growth in this area are higher than for the industry as a whole.

Composing music for games changed profoundly as gaming platforms evolved to incorporate sophisticated multitrack sound playback microchips, more powerful processors, more memory, and built-in DVD players. Today, the power of videogame platforms rivals that of personal computers and, in some respects, surpasses it.

## CONSOLE PLATFORMS

The Nintendo Game Cube has 40 MB of RAM, and Ethernet connectivity to the Internet, and uses an IBM Power PC chip. The game cube has a 3-inch DVD player that's incompatible with commercial music CDs and movie DVDs, but is adequate for storing music files. Its Macronix digital signal processor (DSP) can process up to sixty-four audio channels simultaneously at a 48 kHz sample rate.

**Fig. 7.3.** Nintendo GameCube

The Sony Playstation 2 (PS2) has 32 MB of RAM, and has available accessories to be used as a computer, including a keyboard, mouse, modem, Ethernet, USB, and Linux operating system. It can play commercial CDs and DVDs and can process sixty-four audio channels simultaneously at 44.1 or 48 kHz sample rates.

**Fig. 7.4.** Sony Playstation 2 (PS2)

The Microsoft XBox platform is also a complete computer, running a slim version of the Windows operating system. This allows it to use Windows DirectMusic and DirectSound formats. DirectMusic is a version of MIDI that allows for downloadable sounds (DLS) to be triggered and specified within the MIDI data. This enables MIDI-triggered sample playback, in which samples can be instrument sounds or complete sequences (see later in this chapter). DirectMusic also supports two methods of synthesis: hardware synthesis, in which the device hardware creates the audio, and software synthesis, in which the device's processor creates the audio waveforms. See the appendix for more information on hardware and software synthesis, as well as the various MIDI protocols in common use.

**Fig. 7.5.** Microsoft XBox

## EXERCISE 7.3. HOME CONSOLE GAMES

1. In the Games section of your exercise notebook, start a subsection for home console videogames.
2. Watch gamers playing at least three different home console games.
3. Make notes about how music is used in:

   • the splash screen
   • the startup screen
   • different levels and modes of play
   • transitions between modes or levels of play
   • achieving an objective, such as moving to the next level, defeating an enemy, or solving a puzzle

3. Do you notice any differences in how the music is used compared to arcade games?
4. Play the games yourself. Note how you react to the music, paying particular attention to the emotional impact of the music and the functions it serves, such as indicating which mode and level of play you're in.

## COMPUTER GAMING

Computers begin with a big edge over home videogame consoles. They readily connect to the Internet with included software; they read CDs, CD-ROMs, and DVDs; and they have much higher screen resolutions than televisions, at least 1024 x 768 pixels. In comparison, consoles don't come with Web browsers, even if they have network connections. They can't read consumer-burned CD-ROMs, and their television screens rarely reach the maximum resolution of only 640 x 480 pixels. Computers have keyboards, so if you connect to the Internet or to other players, it's easy to exchange files because you can quickly type their names. Using a game controller for this function is awkward and slow. Lastly, a computer user already owns the microprocessor and screen hardware, so there's no need to buy a console. You just buy the software.

Well, sort of.

Here's the other side of the computer coin. Music playback quality is usually poor unless you purchase outboard powered speakers and an add-in sound card for a PC. That adds cost to the computer setup. The computer keyboard and mouse are adequate for non-real-time strategy games, but less satisfactory for games that require quick reflex actions and the simultaneous control of onscreen navigation and character actions. Console and arcade game controllers, with their buttons and joysticks, are much superior in this regard.

## DIFFERENCES FOR COMPOSERS

The same game, developed for a home gaming console and a computer, presents similar creative challenges to a composer, from the standpoint of attractor screens, transitions, achievement segments, and the like. However, the technology of each platform for playing back music is significantly different in ways that affect the creation of the music score.

Chief among the technology issues is the lack of dedicated multitrack audio DSP chips in computers. Although computers may have the most powerful processors of all the gaming platforms, these are not optimized for video or audio playback, as they are in console DSPs. While game consoles can process (mix and EQ) forty or more audio tracks simultaneously in hardware, computers can be counted on only for a stereo pair, so composers are more limited with their composition options on computers than they are on console games.

On the plus side, computers have much larger RAM capacities than consoles and have hard disks available for storing audio, video, and other files, while consoles lack this built-in hardware.

The result is a trade-off in capabilities, which can influence and possibly constrain a composer's ability to create the same type of score for both computer and console game. The console may have more interactive music features because of its audio track-layering capabilities, but a computer game developer can place additional music files (that don't fit on the CD or DVD) on the Web server, for download to the computer before the game begins.

Since the software program that runs a computer game is compatible with Windows, Mac OS, or Linux, it's likely that a composer can obtain a copy of the program from the game producer and test the music tracks while playing the actual game during the development cycle. The same facility will generally be unavailable for a console game, since it requires a specialized development environment, based on the proprietary console hardware.

## EXERCISE 7.4. COMPUTER GAMES

1. In the Games section in your exercise notebook, start a subsection for computer gaming.
2. Watch gamers playing at least three different computer games.
3. Make notes about how music is used in:

   - the splash screen
   - the startup screen
   - different levels and modes of play
   - transitions between modes or levels of play
   - achieving an objective, such as moving to the next level, defeating an enemy, or solving a puzzle

4. Do you notice any differences in how the music is used compared to arcade and home console games?
5. Play the games yourself. Note how you react to the music, paying particular attention to the emotional impact of the music and the functions it serves, such as indicating which mode and level of play you're in.

## PLATFORM TARGET AUDIENCES

Each of the platforms appeals to different age groups. Young kids (five- to eight-year-olds) usually are less adept at operating computers and are attracted to game consoles because they're easy to use and located near a television set rather than in a home office (computer) setting. Consoles also have multiple controllers so that friends can join in the play. Computer gaming is attractive to teenagers and young adults because they are experienced with using computers at school and work. This group is more engaged by intellectually stimulating games such as simulations and roleplaying, which don't rely as much on hand controllers.

As a composer, you need to be aware of the target audience for both the game platform and the specific title you're working on.

This information can assist you in stylistic and thematic choices, as well as decisions concerning the musical complexity and sophistication. Remember that young kids, teens, young adults, adults, and seniors tend to have significantly different tastes in music.

## GAME MUSIC AUTHORING

Early videogame manufacturers used their own proprietary music creation software. This made sense, since each game used different electronic circuitry, and only those musical sounds and levels of polyphony (number of single instrument tracks) in a specific game's hardware were available to the soundtrack composer. The same was true for the video and animation tools.

Authoring systems were usually created for each game. This was costly and time-consuming, and resulted in programs that were poorly documented and had less than ideal interfaces for composers. Consequently, early game soundtrack composers were usually computer coders who could program the games' sound engines and synthesizers using the same computer languages that the animators and designers used.

Standard formats, such as AIFF, WAV, and MP3, weren't used because they took up too much storage and processing. Even today, game consoles use audio formats such as ADPCM and MIDI/DLS2, which are more compact than but not compatible with AIFF, WAV, and MP3 standards.

As noted earlier, the level of polyphony was originally monophonic—just one note or sound at a time. This capability gradually increased to two, then to three, and then six-voice polyphony. The twenty-first century brought almost unlimited polyphony. Similarly, the textures of sounds that could be generated were originally limited to a few beeps and boops, then expanded to include crude music synthesizer sounds. Eventually, it became possible to include recognizable emulations of acoustic instruments such as strings, woodwinds, brass, and percussion, and finally sample playback of real instruments and orchestral recordings.

Technical issues for digital music are particularly important if games are to be made available on more than one platform. A composer faced with providing a music soundtrack for a particular title that will be developed for many platforms, such as Xbox,

Nintendo 64, PSP, and Macintosh computers, will have to deal with very different capabilities and limitations in each case.

Console game companies still tightly control the authoring software for their platforms. If you wish to create a title for a Nintendo or Microsoft game platform, you will need to purchase a proprietary and expensive authoring system. There are no retail versions available from third parties. Many games are developed in-house with music composed by staff or contracted composers, so that all music rights belong to the manufacturer.

Since there is no general and inexpensive authoring application for composers to learn and practice on, such as PowerPoint for presentations or HTML for the Web, composers have come up with authoring substitutes that, while not perfect, allow music to be triggered interactively and synchronized with videogame screens for auditioning purposes.

The following method is used by many professionals and can be adapted for students and entry-level composers.

## SAMPLE SEQUENCERS FOR AUDITIONING SOUNDTRACKS

Sequencers and samplers were explained in chapter 2, and now we'll explore how you can demo, mock up, or temp your music ideas for games using a sequencer and sampler. This method gets around the problem of needing access to and learning how to use specific console authoring systems for each project.

Every sequencer allows you to assign a track to a particular instrument. Instrument tracks can contain MIDI information or audio recordings. For this technique, we use a hybrid known as sample playback—playing an audio recording that's triggered by a MIDI note. This requires having either a hardware sampler/workstation, such as those manufactured by Roland, Yamaha, and Korg, or a software sampler that may be built-in or external to the sequencer, such as the EXS 24 in Logic, Gigasampler, or Reason.

The instrument track in this case is really a control track that contains MIDI notes, each of which plays a complete audio recording that the composer has made of a music soundtrack sequence. Playing a key on an attached MIDI keyboard or software keyboard triggers the recorded music sequence.

Setting up a sampler to assign and play audio recordings is straightforward, similar to setting up a sampler to play individual drum recordings that make up a drum kit. In both cases, the sampler must be set to "not transpose" the recordings based on which key is struck. With this setting, each key determines which sound recording is triggered, not the pitch at which an instrument sound is triggered.

The following illustration is typical of such a hardware or software sampler assignment.

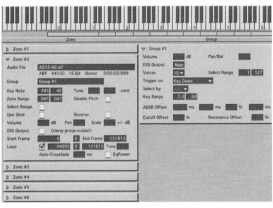

**Fig. 7.6.** Sampler Key Assignment

In the Sampler Key Assignment illustration, the settings for Zone 2 are visible on the left. Zone 2, one of the six zones assigned, is simply a range of keys: D#1 to G#1. You can set the key range to any key(s) that you wish to use to trigger a music file. The name of the music file that has been assigned to these keys is **A033-42.aif**.

If "one shot" were checked, the music file would not loop. Since it is not checked, the looping options are available. These include the starting and ending frame of the loop, which are set to the first and last frame of the music file by default, and the Auto Crossfade option, which automatically crossfades the end and start of the looped music file every time the loop repeats.

The last part of preparing for this method of auditioning is to get a video (or capture a video) of the game that you're working on, with scene changes at points that indicate a player's possible interaction. The video must be loaded into your sequencer as explained in chapter 4, "Previewing Music and Images Together."

## EXERCISE 7.5. AUDITIONING MUSIC WITH VIDEO

Using the method above, audition music sequences with interactive games:

1. Create the sequences you want to audition, and save them as music audio files (AIFF, WAV, or MP3). You also can assemble music files that have been created by others.
2. Assign each music file to a key or key range of your sampler.
3. Load a video of the game into your sequencer.
4. Play your keyboard to trigger the appropriate music sequences assigned to the sampler while you watch the video.

If you can't get a video of the game to work with, you can still use a rough script and try out different sequence transitions in real time.

## EXERCISE 7.6. MOCK UP A GAME SOUNDTRACK

1. Load the video named **WumpasWorld.mov**, on the included CD in the folder **07_Game**, into your sequencer.
2. Set up a sampler key assignment for four zones using the music files on the included CD in the folder **07_Game**, in the subfolder **SamplerMusicZones**. The files are named **MusicZone1.wav**, **MusicZone2.wav**, **MusicZone3.wav**, and **MusicZone4.wav**.
3. Play the video and trigger the music sequences in various patterns to hear and see how well they work.

## WHAT'S NEXT?

Now that we've discussed the basics of composing for videogames, it's time to examine specific videogame genres and discuss how these affect the music you compose. The next chapter details the categories of games and explains how you should approach their soundtracks.

CHAPTER

# 8

# GAME PROCESS AND GENRES

It's important to be able to communicate your ideas with your game production team members. It's helpful to have a clear plan of how you'll go about your soundtrack composition and an understanding of why some games have been successful while others have failed. The former requires an understanding of the process and the latter an understanding of genres.

# PROCESS

Gordon Durity, composer of many film and videogame soundtracks, is senior audio director at Electronic Arts, a leading videogame producer. He outlines the general process of game soundtrack composing as follows:

1. Review the basic imagery—what the visuals will look like.
2. Review the basic story—what the game is about. These first two elements are usually combined in a "storyboard and requirements" document, akin to a comic book that outlines key scenes, actions, and descriptions.
3. Find out the number of music cues required, the length of each scene (sometimes called a "match"), and the aggregate amount of memory available for all the music's audio, MIDI, and sample files.
4. Find out the formats for delivering the soundtrack— usually eight stem tracks—allocated among rhythm/ percussion, lead/melody, harmony/secondary lines, pads/ strings, and specials (instruments/sounds that vary from game to game). Find out whether you need to deliver mono, stereo, or surround-sound stems.
5. Identify the key points in the story arc that will require special musical attention, such as reaching thresholds, winning battles, advancing to next levels, or game suspension while the gamer sets parameters in a window. These outline the general story arc (see chapter 1).
6. For each primary game character, mock up (demo) music for each of the key story points. Typically, a lead character might require sixty-five music cues.
7. Work interactively with your production colleagues, revising and refining your mock-ups until you get approval.
8. Compose the soundtrack cues.
9. Deliver the raw Pro Tools session (the industry-standard format) plus the individual music stems.

# GENRES

Videogames are categorized by genres. This helps gamers sort through the many titles to find their favorite kind of game. It also helps them connect with a community of like-minded gamers. Genre categories focus videogame creative and marketing teams on appropriate features, customers, and player expectations. Game composers should know the basic game genres and be able to refer to illustrative titles as necessary.

The Web portal Yahoo maintains twenty-five genre divisions in its videogame section. Mark J. P. Wolf, in his book *The Medium of the Videogame*, details more than forty. I've collapsed the many possible genres into just a few major categories, with subgenres grouped within. Although each individual game requires its own musical approach, the musical requirements in each major category tend to be similar.

## TWITCH (ACTION) GAMES

Twitch games are generally action-oriented and require quick reflexes. The music soundtracks are similar to those found in action movies, guided by the target player age group, generally teenaged boys. This category is sometimes called action/adventure, but role-playing games (see later) can also be considered adventures, and these are not necessarily twitch games, so it's clearer to stick with twitch and action nomenclature.

Twitch soundtracks usually feature strong rhythmic beats and killer sound effects.

Composers should consider the emotional states of the players as well as the onscreen events. In general, tension and suspense are interspersed with adrenalin rushes and emotional releases. Tempos are usually medium to fast.

Like action movies, twitch games cater strongly to young male audiences. Anthropologists explain this appeal as a substitute for the hunting and tribal warfare to which boys and young men are genetically disposed. The same theory explains the success of gathering-type games, such as *Pac-Man*, with female audiences.

Twitch game subgenres:

- **Capture, catch, and collect**. The player captures escaping, moving, or stationary objects. Examples include *Gopher, Take the Money and Run, Fishing Derby*, and *Pac-Man*, respectively. These games generally appeal to both genders.

- **Combat**. Two or more players shoot projectiles at each other in a fight. One player could be the videogame. Examples include *American Army, Battletech, Nightmare*, and *Warlords*.

- **Dodge**. The player(s) must successfully avoid objects, with scoring determined by the number of objects dodged. Examples include *Dodge 'Em, Frogger*, and *Journey Escape*.

- **Drive, fly, or race**. One of the most traditional genres. The player has the driver's view of a vehicle, racing against other drivers or sometimes just time opponents. Examples include *Gran Tourismo, Mario Kart, Outrun, Indy 500, Night Driver, Pole Position*, and *Street Racer*.

- **Fighting**. The player controls an onscreen battler in hand-to-hand, one-on-one combat. Examples include *Street Fighter, Body Slam, Boxing*, and *Mortal Kombat*.

- **Obstacle course**. The player must cross a difficult path strewn with obstacles, often running and jumping to avoid dangers. Examples include *Super Mario, Donkey Kong, Sonic the Hedgehog, Pitfall!*, and *Jungle Hunt*.

- **Shooter**. The player has many opponents and harmful objects attacking at the same time. Some shooter games are "first person," seen from the perspective of the player's/character's eyes. Some are "third person," usually a perspective behind the shooter. Some games let the player toggle the viewpoint. Shooter games in which the scenes scroll from top to bottom of the screen are sometimes called "shmups," short for "shoot-'em-ups." Examples include *Doom, Halo, Quake*, and the old-time favorites *Space Invaders, Galaxian*, and *Centipede*.

- **Sport**. Adaptations of real-world sports or variations of them. These require physical dexterity to control the athletes in real time, but like many other twitch games, they also rely heavily on strategy. Videogame versions of professional sports like basketball, football, and wrestling are likely to use existing (licensed) or custom-composed pop songs, like those played when goals are scored and at halftime entertainments at pro sporting events. Song styles tend to feature rap, dance, and heavy metal. Sports with less contact, such as tennis and baseball, use less vigorous music. Examples include *Madden NFL*, *NHL Hockey*, *Battle Ping Pong*, *Hot Shots Tennis*, *Pong*, *Skeet Shoot*, and *Tsuppori Sumo Wrestling*.

## EXERCISE 8.1. COMPOSE A TWITCH GAME MUSIC SCORE

Choose one of the twitch game subgenres. Compose a score for a hypothetical game that includes individual cues for the following scene types:

1. Attractor (loop)
2. Startup Screen
3. Situation 1 (loop)
4. Situation 2 (loop)
5. Situation 3 (loop)
6. Success
7. Failure
8. Ultimate Success
9. Ultimate Failure
10. Credits

Name your music files **Twitch.wav** (the musical sequence linking all the individual cues), **TwitchAttractor.wav**, **TwitchStartup.wav**, **TwitchSituation1.wav**, **TwitchSituation2.wav**, and so on. Save the music files in the **Games** subfolder of your **DemoMusic** folder.

## ROLE-PLAYING GAMES (RPGs)

RPGs allow the player to create or take on a character whose personality and attributes (species, race, gender, occupation) and abilities (strength, energy, defense, dexterity) are represented by numerical values. These attributes increase or decrease according to the player's success in the game. The player is an adventurer with combat and magical skills. The objective is generally a noble cause, such as saving a princess or slaying a dragon.

RPG objectives are completed in several steps. The player usually needs to find objects or information in one game location or level that will be required later in other locations or levels—e.g., keys to unlock doors or chests. Like strategy games (see later), the RPG genre requires strategic thinking, but uniquely adds a strong story line and characters that are absent or less important in other game genres.

RPGs are essentially story and character driven. They fit well with the dramatic arc models and compositional techniques discussed in chapter 3, "Musical Identities," and chapter 4, "Functional Music." RPG composers use lots of musical themes, leitmotifs, and functional music techniques.

Music soundtracks for RPG games are usually very different from their twitch game relatives. Instead of rhythmic and bombastic pop stylings, RPG scores tend to use orchestral music stylings. Frequently, the main music theme mirrors the heroic or monumental story theme of the RPG, emphasizing its adventure over its action. For some RPGs, such as *Myst*, the music scores emphasize beauty, rather than majesty. The use of traditional instruments rather than synths is the rule in most cases.

RPG music soundtracks have become so expertly composed that symphony orchestras around the world are devoting concerts to game music, in much the same way they got on the bandwagon for film music a few decades earlier.

The *Zelda* series of videogames is one of the all-time most successful RPGs—more than forty million sold. These have wonderful musical scores, and in some cases integrate the music soundtrack into the storyline. For example, in the *Legend of Zelda: Ocarina of Time*, a musical theme, played by the lead character on an ocarina (flute-like instrument), is a story thread throughout the game.

RPG subgenres:

- **Adventures and quests**. The player navigates through multiple, connected rooms or scenes, each of which may be associated with an objective(s) to fulfill before the player is permitted to move on to other rooms and/or levels. Settings are frequently related to historical eras, science fiction, or fantasy. Examples include *Final Fantasy*, *Ultima*, *Baldur's Gate*, *Adventure*, *Krull*, *Raiders of the Lost Ark*, *Diablo*, and *Star Wars*.

- **Dungeons**. Players are devotees of the original *Dungeons and Dragons* game. Gary Gygax and David Arneson, the creators of *D&D*, first published the game in 1974. The authors borrowed heavily from the fictional mythologies of J.R.R. Tolkien (*Lord of the Rings*), Edgar Rice Burroughs (*Pellucidar*), and Michael Moorcock (*Elric*), as well as Norse mythology. The roleplaying was modeled on historic European war games in which onlookers were allowed to participate by playing relevant characters during the battle. *D&D* has about twenty million players worldwide and has sold more than a billion dollars' worth of books and equipment. It is credited with spawning the entire subsequent genre of RPG videogames. *Warcraft* is a notable example of an RPG in the *D&D* mold.

- **Modeling**. Players tend to be female, outfitting an onscreen character associated with the player, known as an "avatar," with a wardrobe of clothing and accessories. The avatar can choose a pet, go on an adventure, and populate the game world with appropriate accessories. The archetypal game is *Barbie: Fashion Designer*, released in 1996. Many modeling games are true RPGs, while others are primarily shopping inducements. There is a fine line between the two, particularly for female audiences who might view shopping as an entertainment. The most popular titles relate to the Barbie franchise, such as *Barbie: Fashion Designer, Barbie's Horse Adventures,* and *Secret Agent Barbie.*

- **Myst type**. Players are devotees of the original *Myst* game. Created by Rand and Robyn Miller in 1993, *Myst* and its sequels topped the sales charts for many years, selling more than twelve million copies. It was the first adventure videogame to incorporate extremely high quality and beautiful visual images and music. As evidence of the high regard that the creators hold for *Myst's* soundtrack, they included a music CD of the score along with the game—a first for the industry. *Myst* defies many of the conventions of adventure gaming: you don't die, there's no graphical interface, you don't have to use a controller or look down at the keyboard, and there are no complicated menus. The *Myst* phenomenon brought many new players into the fold and crossed demographic and gender boundaries. Examples include *Riven*, *Exile*, *Revelation*, *End of Ages*, and *Uru*.

- **Multiplayer Online RPG Games: MUDs, MOOs, and MUSHs.** These networked RPG games, called MUDs (Multi-User Dungeons), MOOs (MUD, Object Oriented), and MUSHs (Multi-User Shared Hallucination), provide a virtual online environment where many players can log on and interact with each other, providing a social commons as well as a gaming experience. Instead of the recommended seven-player limit for the pencil and paper *D&D* game, MUDs accommodate up to fifty or more players within a single game, because mainframe host computers are powerful enough to handle the load.

  In a MUD, each player takes control of a computerized persona (avatar) who moves about the space, chats with other characters, explores dangerous monster-infested areas, solves puzzles, and even creates new rooms, descriptions, and accessory items. MUDs evolved and added graphics and music, but are still more primitive than MMOGs (see below). Consequently, they require much less computing and network power.

  RPGs were the first games to take advantage of networked multiplayer virtual spaces enabled by the Internet. The early Internet offered a perfect platform to host RPGs, because players could connect at low modem speeds for the necessary text; no complex graphics or sounds were required. This was and continues to be particularly important for players in with unsophisticated network access and computer facilities. Examples include *Zork* and *Online Dungeons and Dragons*.

- **Massively Multiplayer RPG Games (MMOGs).** MUDs, MOOs, and MUSHs evolved into MMOGs and their subset **MMORPGs** (Massively Multiplayer Online Role-Playing Games), which include stunning graphics, animation, video, and high-quality sound and music. The various acronyms are usually aggregated into the general category of MMOs (Massively Multiplayer Onlines).

While MUDs rely on host computers for the computational muscle, MMOs commandeer the power and storage available in home computers. That shifts the image and sound-processing load to the player's computer, requiring the host server to manage only the lower-bandwidth user interactions and non-real-time downloads. Music plays a much more critical role in these games, which feature rich acoustic orchestral scores on par with top Hollywood movie scores.

MMOs can be played by huge numbers of players. Games such as *Lineage* have many millions of subscribers and *World of Warcraft* has tens of millions. The number of online players for a single game at any time can be tens or even hundreds of thousands, although these players are generally segmented by the game's software into smaller shards—groups of no more than a few thousand players sharing a single server. Other MOOs include *Ultima Online, Second Life, EverQuest, Anarchy Online, Realm Online*, and *Starcraft*.

## EXERCISE 8.2. COMPOSE AN RPG GAME SCORE

Choose one of the RPG game subgenres. Compose a score for a hypothetical game that includes the following scene types:

1. Attractor (loop)
2. Startup Screen
3. Situation 1 (loop)
4. Situation 2 (loop)
5. Situation 3 (loop)
6. Success
7. Failure
8. Ultimate Success
9. Ultimate Failure
10. Credits

Name your music files **RPG.wav** (the musical sequence linking all the individual cues), **RPGAttractor.wav**, **RPGStartup.wav**,

**RPGSituation1.wav**, **RPGSituation2.wav**, and so on. Save the music files in the **Games** subfolder of your **DemoMusic** folder.

## STRATEGY GAMES

Strategy videogames emphasize mental rather than physical skills. Sometimes, strategy games can be applied to military situations, but for the most part, the main objective is to figure out a solution or best move, rather than to prevail over an enemy or obstacles. Strategy games often involve solving problems that may be spatial, such as finding paths and manipulating objects. Many strategy games mirror a real-world game counterpart or are inspired by one, particularly board, card, and gambling games.

The music for strategy games is as varied as the games themselves, allowing a composer to choose from a wide range of styles. In general, strategy games use music that is less dramatic than that used in RPGs and twitch games. Instead of alternating scenes of tension and action, strategy games lend themselves to more constant and laid-back musical styles—more like radio and elevator music than movie scores. Styles are more likely to be easy rock, country, smooth jazz, ambient, or the like. Some strategy videogames allow the player to select from a catalog of music, usually in a drop-down menu, or to mute the music.

Games adopted from television programs, such as *Jeopardy*, benefit from licensing the well-known television music themes associated with the show. Composers are cautioned to respect copyright laws when they create soundtracks that sound similar to existing musical themes without first obtaining copyright licenses.

Strategy game subgenres:

- **Board and card**. These emulate the real-world games they're modeled after, such as chess, checkers, backgammon, *Scrabble*, *Monopoly*, rummy, or solitaire. In addition, they can include features that real-world games cannot offer, such as suggested moves, compilation of high scores, training sessions, and a dummy opponent—the computer.

- **Gambling**. The player bets a stake of virtual money (or real money, if it's an online casino Web site), which increases or decreases the player's assets. All real-world gambling casino games have been made available as videogames, including poker, blackjack, roulette, craps, and slot machines.

- **Puzzles**. Graphical enigmas like *Rubik's Cube* and word puzzles such as crosswords, word searches, and anagrams have many iterations available as videogames.

- **Mazes**. The player must successfully navigate onscreen to an endpoint while avoiding physical barriers. When these games are in real time, such as *Pac-Man*, they cross over to the action/obstacle subgenre of twitch games. Examples include *Descent, Maze Craze, Tunnel Runner,* and *Take the Money.*

- **Quizzes**. The main objective of quiz games is to successfully answer questions. Some quiz games, like *Trivial Pursuit* and *Name That Tune*, are adaptations of board and television games. Others, such as *Wizz Quiz, You Don't Know Jack,* and *NFL Football Trivia Challenge*, have been created specifically for the genre.

## EXERCISE 8.3. COMPOSE A STRATEGY GAME SCORE

Choose one of the strategy game subgenres. Compose a score for a hypothetical game that includes the following scene types:

1. Attractor (loop)
2. Startup Screen
3. Situation 1 (loop)
4. Situation 2 (loop)
5. Situation 3 (loop)
6. Success
7. Failure
8. Ultimate Success
9. Ultimate Failure
10. Credits

Name your music files **Strategy.wav** (the musical sequence linking all the individual cues), **StrategyAttractor.wav**, **StrategyStartup.wav**, **StrategySituation1.wav**, **StrategySituation2.**

**wav**, and so on. Save the music files in the **Games** subfolder of your **DemoMusic** folder.

# SIMULATION GAMES (SIMS)

Sim games try to simulate the real world as closely as possible, instead of creating fantasies or alternate realities. Sims are open-ended and noncombative, and emphasize construction over destruction. From this perspective, they are the antithesis of action and adventure games. Sims don't necessarily have objectives or endings. They combine strategic thinking with "what if I were God" scenarios to construct and populate communities according to the wishes of the player and, in the process, provide unique entertainments. You can't win in the usual sense, although you can lose, if you run out of money or resources, or if you starve your characters to death.

The Sim category is based on the classic groundbreaking SimCity game, designed by Will Wright for his company Maxis, published for the Commodore computer in 1987, and then distributed for Mac and PC platforms in 1989. The Sim game series has sold more than thirty million units, one of the highest-selling computer games ever.

Sim games combine strategy with immersive personal experiences. It's not surprising, then, that some music cues for Sims are similar to strategy game music, while others are similar to RPG music. Some music soundtracks may be ambient while others are dramatic, suspenseful, or action oriented.

There's an additional type of game music in Sims called "source." Source music is used frequently in movies, when the source of music is onscreen or implied. This is different than the score type of music cues we have been dealing with. Examples of source music include a car radio, a stereo system, or a piano player in a bar. Since Sims emulate real-life situations, they tend to include television sets, iPods, and such. They can also take place in nightclubs, dance clubs, opera houses, pubs, and restaurants where music is being played. In these environments, the game music and its production quality should reflect the music that's shown or implied in the scene.

Sim games are popular with many players who don't like twitch or RPG. However, older twitch and RPG gamers frequently migrate to Sim games and find them compelling. Sim creator

Wright notes, "My games are more like a hobby—a train set or a dollhouse." [Keighley, Geoff. "SIMply Divine." www.gamespot.com (August 2006).]

Sim game subgenres:

- **Resource Management Sims**. Players balance the use of limited resources to build or expand a community, institution, or empire, while dealing with problems such as crime, pollution, and natural disasters. Examples include *SimCity*, *SimFarm*, *SimAnt*, *SimEarth*, *Aerobiz*, *Caesar II*, *Civilization*, *M.U.L.E*, *SimTower*, and *Spaceward Ho!*

- **Social Sims**. Virtual people, also called Sims, take their generic name from the game genre. The original ground-breaking game, *The Sims,* was released in 2000 as a follow-on to Maxim's *SimCity* game series. It was an immediate hit. The player is in control of a virtual house and/or larger community, controlling the daily activities of the residents. These activities may include sleeping, eating, cooking, bathing, socializing, and so on. If the Sims don't get enough rest and nourishment, they sicken and die. The Sims' financial needs and career goals are variable, as well.

  Players can optionally give the Sims characters free will, in which case their actions are based in part on the player's input, and in part on characteristics set for them, for objects in their environment, and for events that are transpiring. So, as a character approaches a chair, for example, the chair communicates with the character about its proximity, and it influences but does not compel the character toward sitting down.

  The only real objective of the game is to organize the time of the Sims so they can reach their personal advancement goals. Examples include *The Sims*, *The Sims 2*, *URBZ*, and *The Sims Bustin' Out.*

- **The Sims Online**. This is a MMOG that merges *SimCity* and *The Sims* into a massively multiplayer game. You install the game, set up your account, log on, download the obligatory patches, and pick your avatar. *The Sims Online* is probably one of the friendliest newbie games, with rewards for players that create attractive scenarios. If a player creates an interesting house that attracts many visitors, they earn Sim money that allows them to create more game items.

## INSTRUCTIONAL GAMES

Instructional videogames are designed to teach or train the player. The expected outcomes of a session are both education and entertainment. For this reason, these games are sometimes called "edutainment." The entertainment value, usually provided by music and animation, creates a more positive attitude toward learning for the player/student and has been shown to greatly increase the retention of information.

The Web site www.worldwidelearn.com offers 352 subject areas from hundreds of institutions that use edutainment for their courses. Instructional games are particularly effective for children, who view them as playtime activities, with learning as an important but incidental bonus.

The music for edutainment games varies according to the scenarios used by the creators. Some titles are based on strategy games, some on RPG, others on action, and yet others on simulations. In each case, the music cues tend to mirror music cues used in the emulated game genre.

Instructional videogames are available as stand-alone programs or as part of online courses offered by schools, colleges, universities, and training institutions. Examples include *Mario's Early Years*, *Fun with Numbers*, *Math Blaster*, *Carmen Sandiego*, *Mavis Beacon Teaches Typing*, the *Oregon Trail* series, and *Robocode*.

## MUSIC AND DANCE

These arcade games require players to keep time with a musical rhythm, either by tapping a controller (which may be drum-like, turntable-like, maracas-like, or guitar-like) or by stepping on foot actuators. Examples include *Dance Dance Revolution*, *Beatmania*, *Bust a Groove*, *DrumMania*, *Guitar Freaks*, *PaRappa the Rapper*, *Pop 'n' Music*, *Samba de Amigo*, and *Um Jammer Lammy*.

## WHAT'S NEXT?

Thus far, we've dealt with interactive media in presentations and arcades, and on computers and game consoles. But what if you want to access interactive media on the go? The next chapter is about mobile media—portable game consoles, PIMs, Pocket PCs, and mobile phones. Many believe that these will be the most popular interactive media in the future.

CHAPTER

# 9

# MOBILE MEDIA MUSIC

In the twentieth century, music was mostly attached to stationary devices: radios, televisions, and stereos. This required users to move to the devices in order to use them. In the twenty-first century, music will be mostly in portable devices—iPods, Palms, Game Boys, and cell phones. Now music can be attached to users, wherever they are, even while they're moving.

## MOBILE AND PORTABLE MEDIA

While portable media, such as home gaming consoles and laptop computers, can be easily taken from place to place, mobile media can be used while moving from place to place. Mobile media that are interactive include cellular and satellite phones, personal information managers (PIMs), portable gaming consoles, and hand-held personal music and video players.

Current devices are changing, though, as each device category spawns hybrids that mirror many capabilities of other device categories. There are cellphones available with digital camera, gaming, PIMs, and music playback functions; PIMs with digital cameras, wireless communications, and gaming functions; music players with PIMs, video playback, and computer-like operating systems; and portable gaming consoles with music and video players, wireless communications, and PIM functions.

As a result, mobile media are converging into a single large category that encompasses the previously distinct industries of telephony, home entertainment, gaming, and consumer electronics.

The move to mobile is happening everywhere and in all segments of society. Children use their Play Station Portables (PSPs) and Nintendo DSs while they ride in buses or cars. Mobile phones are increasingly used as alternatives to tethered home and office telephones. BlackBerrys, Palms, and Pocket PCs are connecting to the Web through Wi-Fi and cellular networks to receive and send e-mails in coffee shops and business meetings. And personal music and video players are starting to replace stereos and televisions as entertainment devices—ones you can use at home and then take with you as you travel.

No matter what their original category, new mobile media devices all are capable of receiving and storing music, on its own or married with visual images as interactive media, including presentations, Web pages, and games.

Mobile media share certain technical limitations that affect their storage and playback of music. Composers need to understand these in order to maximize the quality of the scores they create.

# COMPOSING FOR MOBILE MEDIA

Composing music for mobile media applications that are similar to applications on fixed media, such as presentations, Web pages, and games, uses many of the same skills as for fixed media. But there are important differences in the technologies of music storage and distribution for mobile devices that require significant adjustments for the composer, and in many cases, more complicated and time-consuming planning and production.

In addition, there are specific musical applications such as ringtones (short music that's synthesized in the device) and song-tones (recordings of song excerpts), also called ringtones, which are unique to mobile media. New mobile applications are catching on, such as short animations, videos, and dramatic series. Each of these requires its own musical treatment and will, no doubt, evolve its own musical grammar of usage.

Mobile devices are significantly different from fixed media in terms of audio playback and the environment in which music is listened to. If you produce a music soundtrack for a portable device the same way you do for a fixed media device, the music will likely sound thin and musical subtleties will be lost, because the frequency and dynamic ranges of portable amp/speaker combinations are very limited. In addition, mobile environments such as trains, cars, and buses have higher ambient noise levels that can mask the soft portions of dynamic musical passages.

One solution to these problems is to compress the finished music so that its dynamic range is smaller and better suited to the limited dynamic range of the mobile device's playback system. This makes the music seem louder and turns some nuances into prominent features, so adjustments for this must be made in the composition.

A second trick is to double low-frequency bass lines an octave higher, such as pairing cellos with basses or guitars with bass guitars. This will make the bottom end more noticeable and stronger. Similarly, equalization of low-end instruments such as bass drums should be emphasized in the 100–250 Hz region instead of the more fundamental 20–50 Hz region.

These methods come with their own problems, particularly during this time of technology transition. If you plug a portable unit's sound output into a home theater or computer with a decent set of outboard amplifiers and speakers, the compressed and equalized music sounds less dynamic and at a lower fidelity than the comparable scores would sound on a full-size gaming console or computer.

This situation is similar to the one that composers found themselves in when home theaters were first introduced. Compressed and midrange-heavy music scores that sounded great on normal television sets sounded lifeless and lo-fi on home theater setups. Music written and produced with full cinematic dynamics and frequency range sounded great on home theaters but sounded thin and obscured on normal TVs.

Around the year 2000, composers began to switch their television soundtrack deliverables to full cinematic quality sound, complete with surround-sound components, for home theaters that could decode it. The rationale of the television production industry was, "If you don't have a home theater yet, you'd better get one if you want to hear decent sound. Otherwise, don't blame us."

In the case of mobile platforms, it's not clear when this switchover will occur. Based on the units available in 2006 and the modes that gamers are using them in, it makes sense to compress your music's frequency and dynamic ranges, in order to keep the music "hot."

## COMPRESSED MUSIC

In the previous chapters, we examined arcade, console, and computer gaming. Each of these interactive media platforms is capable of storing and playing CD-quality recorded music. They all can play CDs and DVDs, which hold hundreds of megabytes and even gigabytes of information—plenty of storage for music. They also have RAM ranging from tens of megabytes to gigabytes, and sometimes hard drives with almost limitless storage.

Mobile platforms lack these capacities. CD and DVD playback is impossible because the small size of mobile media doesn't permit the inclusion of CD media. The same physical size limitation, as well as limited battery capacities, means that available RAM is much lower as well.

Consequently, mobile media generally rely on a combination of meta-music and highly compressed audio. Both of these formats affect the soundtrack options available to composers.

## META-MUSIC

Meta-music means "information about music." More precisely, meta-music data contains information about music notes (pitches with starting and ending times) and timbres (musical instrument textures) that need to be synthesized by electronics. The most common example of meta-music is MIDI. A device's music synthesizer uses the information about the music to create audio that is played through the unit's built-in or external speakers, earphones, or earbuds.

Meta-music greatly reduces the bandwidth and memory required to transmit and store music. To illustrate its utility, consider the song "Three Blind Mice." Performed at a moderate pace, the melody of "Three Blind Mice" takes about sixteen seconds to sing or play through once. A sound recording of that melody in CD format is more than two megabytes in size. The MIDI representation of the same song, which only contains information about the melody's tempo, notes, and timbres, requires less than two hundred bytes of data, a compression factor of about ten thousand to one (10,000:1).

Thus, the bandwidth required to transmit and store meta-music is much lower than that required to transmit and store sound recordings. It's ideal for low-bandwidth networks like those used for cell phones.

The synthesizer chips in many of the mobile devices are much more limited in their timbral variety than the hardware and software synths in a composer's studio, so composers need to limit their orchestral palette when composing for mobile devices. In addition, mobile device music synthesizers all have fairly low levels of polyphony—the number of simultaneous parts they can play. For example, a synthesizer chip with six-note polyphony can play parts for bass, a melody, drums, and three other parts, sometimes assigned to harmonies and sometimes used for simultaneous drum parts, such as a cymbal and bass drum hitting at the same time.

## EXERCISE 9.1. 6-PART MIDI MUSIC

1. Load the music file **6PartMusic.mid** from the folder **09_Mobile** on the included CD into your sequencer.

2. Assign a different sound to each MIDI part, corresponding to the part's name. Listen to the mix of your MIDI orchestration.

3. Load the audio file **6PartMix.wav** into your sequencer. This is the mix of my MIDI orchestration, intended to sound like a classic *Super Mario*–era music cue, and orchestrated with classic game sounds. Similar sounds and limitations exist in many mobile phones today.

## MIDI FOR MOBILES

The most popular meta-music format used for non-mobile devices is the Musical Instrument Digital Interface (MIDI). Plain-vanilla MIDI orchestration only contains numeric information about which instrument should play each musical part, called a "track." Each sound number is called a "patch," a remnant of the old days when analog synthesizers had patch cords connected between electronic modules to produce an instrument sound. Each synthesizer that reproduces that part interprets a MIDI patch number, such as 98 in bank 4, differently depending on which sound is in bank 4 sound 98.

General MIDI (GM) was introduced to allow a standard set of sounds to be available on many different synthesizers, so that composers could be confident that MIDI patch 1 would sound like a piano, MIDI patch 25 like a guitar, and so on.

Still, you never can know the exact instrument sound or volume that a synthesizer will make from a GM file, since different synthesizers produce very different types of sounds.

To get around this difficulty, the DownLoadable Sound (DLS) protocol was developed. It allows a composer to associate an instrument sample (recording) with each MIDI patch number. The instrument sample is loaded into the synthesizer's memory before playback and continues to be used for that patch number. So, patch 1 might be associated with a specific out-of-tune honky-tonk piano, say, rather than just the default MIDI piano in program 1.

This scheme worked pretty well for home gaming consoles, but mobile devices have less powerful processors and less memory, so they can't handle the 32-voice polyphony that GM allows. Several alternative protocols and standards are in use for mobile devices that address this problem.

The MIDI Lite standard cuts the level of polyphony from GM's 32 (24 pitched instruments plus 8 percussion) to 16 (15 pitched instruments plus 1 percussion).

Scalable polyphony MIDI (SP-MIDI) addressed the problem of different mobile devices having different levels of polyphony. In SP-MIDI, the composer specifies the priority level of each MIDI part. When a device lacks the capability of playing all the parts, it discards those with the lowest priority first. This allows a consumer to build a music library in an inexpensive mobile phone that may have only 8-voice polyphony and then, sometime in the future, move the library to a more capable phone with 16- or 32- voice polyphony. It also lets users trade music with friends, who might have mobile phones with different capabilities. Finally, it allows companies who sell music for phones to provide a single file that will work on many different phones.

The eXtensible Music Format (XMF) combines a Standard MIDI File (SMF), which is usually in SP-MIDI, with DLS-formatted samples into a single aggregated file that can be downloaded to a mobile device. Once it's in the phone, the XMF file is disassembled into its component files, which are used for sequencing and instrument sounds.

Mobile phones and other simple devices use a wide variety of other meta-music formats for simple music, such as ringtones. The Ring Tone Text Transfer protocoL (RTTTL) works with many phones. It's a text file that contains the name of the music, the tempo, and the names of each note, along with its duration. The Ring Tone Xfer (RTX) format is the successor to RTTTL, and is compatible with the Short Message Service (SMS) that's used for transferring text to many cell phones, as well as Nokia's Multimedia Messaging Service (MMS). Devices with Yamaha sound chips use the Synthetic Music Mobile Application Format (SMAF). The iMelody protocol includes information about volume, adding dynamic range to melody files. It's used by mobile media that use the Enhanced Message Service (EMS), such as Alcatel, Ericsson, Motorola, and Siemens.

You might wonder if all this technical jargon is necessary in a music composition book. It is. When you're asked to compose or orchestrate music for mobile media, you need to understand the protocols and standards under which it will be distributed and played.

How can you write music if you don't know how many instruments you can use? How can you write music if you don't know what the instruments will sound like? And, how can you write music in a new way with only a guaranteed minimum number of instrument parts plus optional additional parts that may be heard only on certain devices?

The appendix, "Technical Info," deals more completely with music file formats. Please refer to it as necessary.

## COMPRESSED AUDIO

When sound recordings are used in mobile devices, they are frequently compressed for distribution and storage, so they can be transmitted more quickly and take up less memory. There are two types of compression: lossless and lossy. *Lossless* compression yields compression ratios of only about 2:1. *Lossy* compression can compress music recordings from about 10:1 up to 100:1 ratios, while losing a little quality at the lower compression ratio and delivering much lower fidelity at highest compression ratio—hence the term "lossy."

MP3 compression, technically known as MPEG-1 Audio Layer III, became an official standard in 1992 and has been used extensively for compressing content on commercial music for online distribution and exchange. The audio compression standard for MPEG-2 and MPEG-4 coding is called Advanced Audio Coding (AAC). It produces better quality and smaller files than MP3. Many other compression schemes (known as codecs, which is a contraction of **co**de and **dec**ode) have been invented that improve on MP3, such as Ogg Vorbis, APE, and ASF, but MP3 remains the most popular. All lossy compression schemes degrade the sound quality to varying extents.

If a platform uses compressed music, the composer need not make any compromises in orchestration or limitations to polyphony. The formats that a composer delivers for these media types are WAV or AIFF, just as for non-mobile devices. The audio compression is done by the content provider. For mobile games, the sound quality can vary from acceptable to excellent, depending on the model and price range of the mobile platform. For MP3 players, such as the iPod (hard disk) or Sansa (Flash RAM), it's usually excellent.

**Fig. 9.1.** SanDisk Sansa MP3 Player

## PLAYBACK SOUND QUALITY

Playback sound quality is a double-edged sword for portable media. On the one hand, the tiny speakers in these devices deliver very limited frequency response and even more limited dynamic range. On the other hand, portable devices can be listened to through earphones or earbuds that can have better sound fidelity than typical speakers and televisions connected to computers and home consoles.

## MOBILE GAME CONSOLES

Gaming is a popular activity on all mobile media, but dedicated mobile consoles have advantages for game play, notably bigger screen displays and familiar gaming controls. PIMs and cell-phones, in contrast, have displays that are smaller and lower resolution. Their user interfaces and controls are generally inadequate for sophisticated gaming.

The original Game Boy, the classic mobile gaming device, had just four shades of grey in its 160 x 144 pixel screen. Although television screens have fifteen times greater resolution and can display millions of colors, Game Boy's mobility made it a huge and instant success. Thirty-two million Game Boys were sold in its first three years of release. Game Boy has had more than six hundred game titles released for it.

Bundled with the widely popular Russian-designed game *Tetris*, Game Boy changed family traveling culture worldwide. Instead of unhappy and obnoxious kids squirming and squealing in the back seats of automobiles on family outings, there were well-behaved and happy kids playing Game Boys, which made the obnoxious beeping sounds.

Game Boys were incarnations of public desire so well matched to their market that other products have had difficulty competing. This was the case for the first fifteen years of its release, during which Game Boy and its successors Game Boy Pocket, Game Boy Color, and Game Boy Advance ruled the portable gaming market without significant competition, selling about two hundred million units.

The music capabilities of Game Boy Advance, a recent version of this device, are sophisticated and complex. It can play back samples at 32 kHz, 8-bit resolution, as well as perform subtractive synthesis, which filters basic waveforms like an analog synthesizer. In addition, Game Boy Advance also has a unique thirty-two-step loopable wavetable synthesis engine. The memory allocated for samples is very limited, so you have to rely mainly on the synthesized instruments.

The Game Boy Advance hardware includes the ability to play music and games that were created for older models—backward compatibility—while adding additional sound processing capabilities. Still, the lack of sufficient memory and CD playback limits the music soundtracks, which nonetheless must emulate soundtracks that were originally created for home consoles such as the Nintendo 64, Super Nintendo, and Game Cube.

**Fig. 9.2.** Original Game Boy (Left), Game Boy Advance (Right)

The most recent evolution of portable gaming from Nintendo is the DS (for Dual Screen), with a clamshell design. One of the two 3-inch screens is touch-sensitive and works with a stylus—like Palms and Pocket PCs—to control the action in some games. It also serves as a PIM. The DS has Wi-Fi communication to connect with other units for cordless multiplayer gaming and Internet access. Music and sound are handled differently than in Game Boys. The DS has sixteen simultaneous digital audio channels for music and effects, so mixing and matching tracks can be done on the fly, while the game is being played.

The main competition for Nintendo DS is Sony's PlayStation Portable (PSP). The PSP has a wide screen that supports sixteen million colors in a resolution of 480 x 272. PSP's D-Pad and buttons are positioned similarly to its home console PlayStation, and it incorporates stereo speakers, a headphone jack, and volume/brightness controls. It has a Wi-Fi option and USB, which allow multiplayer and online gaming. PSP can play movies and music using Sony's Memory Stick or Universal Media Disk (UMD) hardware. The music formats that are supported are MP3 and Sony's ATRAC3+.

**Fig. 9.3.** Nintendo DS with two screens (Left), Sony PSP—Personal PlayStation (Right)

## PIMS

PIMs are personal information managers. The first and leading manufacturer is Palm, which launched the Palm Pilot in 1996 with the now-standard applications of calendar, address book, to-do list, and notepad. As the category took off in sales and consumer mind-share, additional functions were added to many PIMs, most notably sound playback, a color screen, and video playback capability for games. What started out as a business device has become an entertainment platform. Wireless communications have also been added to certain models, using mobile phone networks or Wi-Fi. Now, PIMs are converging with mobile phones, as these add PIM functions and include larger screens.

An example of this media convergence is the Treo 650 from Palm. Treo is a full-function PIM, cellphone, e-mail application, Web browser, QWERTY keyboard, music player, digital audio recorder, and digital camera in a single unit that can communicate with a wireless headset via Bluetooth. Hundreds of excellent games are available for this platform, many of them versions of popular arcade, console, and computer games. The audio quality is decent because the units have significant built-in RAM and expansion possibilities.

Composers for PIM applications need to learn the particular sound capabilities and operating systems of the target device. Palms, for example, use the Palm OS, with different development tools than those used for mobile phones, Pocket PCs, or portable gaming consoles.

**Fig. 9.4.** Palm Treo 650 with Wireless Headset

## POCKET PCS

Pocket PCs use Microsoft's Windows Pocket PC OS and, optionally, Windows Mobile OS. Since the OS is a version of Windows, Pocket PCs are actually small computers. That means that they can run versions of computer applications such as Word and Excel.

Users can easily and seamlessly upload and download application files between their computer and Pocket PC.

Pocket PCs and PIMs have become almost identical in the minds of consumers. Palm OS, the most popular PIM operating system, now boasts compatibility with Microsoft Word, Excel, and PowerPoint files as well as with other popular computer applications. Pocket PCs, such as the HP iPAQ and Dell Axim series (see illustration), have all the usual PIM software, including calendar, address book, to-do list, and memos, and add Wi-Fi, Bluetooth, e-mail, Web browser, music playback, and game play capability, making them almost indistinguishable from PIM products.

Audio files on Pocket PCs are usually in the Windows Media Audio (WMA) format, which sounds somewhat better than MP3 at low bit rates (smaller files). It also has built-in Digital Rights Management (DRM) to prevent piracy of music files. Like the PIMs, Pocket PCs provide a large variety of games. As the category evolves, these devices will greatly expand their music capabilities by using the DirectMusic and DirectSound formats that are parts of the Windows OS family.

**Fig. 9.5.** Dell Axim X50v (Left), HP Pocket PC (Right)

## SMARTPHONES

Smartphones are cell phones powered by the Windows Mobile Operating System, a close cousin of the Pocket PC OS, offering the same familiar look and feel. While Smartphones aren't generally as powerful or versatile as Pocket PCs, they are lighter and less expensive and have basic PIM functions, as well as mobile phone capability.

With the convergent evolution of these media, however, many Smartphones also have built-in digital cameras, e-mail, Web browsing, music playing, and Bluetooth functions, like Pocket PCs and PIMs. Their gaming is somewhat restricted by small screens, but it is nonetheless an important user activity. Cellphone games generally use music and sound effects playback, although these are limited, because of the phones' smaller memories compared to Pocket PCs and PIMs. Still, if you examine a unit like AudioVox SMT5600 (figure 9.6), it's hard to tell the difference between it and the Pocket PC and PIM devices.

**Fig. 9.6.** AudioVox SMT5600 Smartphone

## WHAT'S NEXT?

This chapter ends part II: The Media. Now that we've gone through the basics in part I, and detailed how composers should treat each interactive media device in part II, it's time to get professional tips about creative judgments, working relationships, and taking care of business. That's what part III is about.

Part **III**

# PROFESSIONAL TIPS

CHAPTER

# 10

## AESTHETICS

After all the craft problems have been solved, after the music functions and production requirements have been met, we're left with matters of art. Aesthetic judgment sets one composer apart from another. Although artistry can't be taught, you can learn to maximize the ability you have.

## MORE OR LESS?

How do you know if your music cues are over-written (too many musical ideas and not enough clarity) or under-written (too thin and cheesy sounding)? Here's a useful test:

**If a musical work is ideal, adding to it or subtracting from it will diminish it.**

Use this principle to quickly test whether you've optimized your music. Try adding and subtracting musical elements or portions of them. Then listen to determine whether or not your music is improved.

Try leaving out part of the rhythm or harmony for a number of bars. Try adding a countermelody. Turn complete tracks on and off. Listen carefully, and determine what they're adding, if anything, to the overall impression of the cue.

Change the orchestration by doubling instrument parts with other instruments. Does this add fatness and impact, or does it detract from the clarity of the part? Try changing the orchestration of a part when it repeats. Try doubling the part and lowering its volume in the mix on the repeat.

Try adding ambience—stringy pads or transparent sounds. If your music is sounding too dense, try eliminating or lowering the level of the pads. Pads sometimes can work best when they're barely audible. If you mix them at too high a level, they can muddy up the cue.

You also can add or subtract entire music sequences in AABAC-format music cues and judge if the sequence sounds better or not.

Bring in a friend or colleague for another opinion.

## ACOUSTIC OR SYNTHETIC INSTRUMENTS

Using live musicians playing acoustic instruments is a recent trend in interactive media. Interactive media previously used mostly synthesized sounds and simple orchestrations with just a few parts, because of limitations in authoring tools, distribution media, playback applications, storage, and budgets.

Nowadays, acoustic orchestrations are common in many interactive media productions. Even when professionals compose synth scores, they frequently bring in a few acoustic instrumentalists to "sell" the music cues. It's amazing how a synth score comes to life when you replace the synth lead with a live oboe, for example, or add a live bass player or guitarist to a rhythm loop.

If you don't have any training in music orchestration and arranging, you should consider getting such training. Alternatively, you should consider hiring an experienced orchestrator to help you in that regard. There's no stigma to using orchestrators. Many of the top Hollywood composers use them regularly.

## GETTING THE STYLE RIGHT

Musical style is one of the most important decisions that a composer must make, yet there's less information and guidance about this aspect of composing than any other area. Even producers, who should have a firm grasp of the stylistic approaches they want for each creative component of the project, frequently have trouble articulating their desired musical style to composers.

The familiar line "I don't know how to describe it, but I'll know when I hear it," can be frustrating for composers. It also can be a blessing, since it gives us free reign to use our personal peaks of expertise, and to use a style that may not have been obvious to the producer but may work well for the project.

Composer Amin Bhatia relates the following anecdote about a conversation he had with a producer:

Amin:       "What about the musical style?"
Producer:   "Absolutely!"
Amin:       "Absolutely what?"
Producer:   "Absolutely, the music must have style."

Here are some tips to help you hone in on an appropriate style:

• Make every effort to get information about the target audience for the presentation. Research the styles of music that they listen to, and use this information to inform your choice of style.

- Investigate interactive media projects similar to yours. Analyze the musical style(s) used. Decide whether you want to be safe and use similar style(s) or break the mold and use a different style. If you decide to take a new approach, be prepared to defend your decision.

## UNITY AND UNIQUENESS

Why do producers hire composers for interactive music projects if they can license library music more cheaply? If you can't answer this question, you probably aren't ready to sell your services to a producer. Here are two major benefits that producers get from original music composers:

- Library music is licensed non-exclusively. The better-quality music libraries tend to be used very frequently, and so a producer will hear the library music that's been licensed for her project in many other projects by different producers. This devalues the uniqueness and impact of a project with library music tracks.

- Licensed music tracks are a hodge-podge of styles, orchestrations, and themes. A commissioned composer can deliver a soundtrack that has *unity* and *coherence*, two very valuable properties that help bring together the elements of a production and leave a focused impression on a user or audience.

Novice composers should pay particular attention to the second point, since many do not take enough care in their composing to ensure that the entire soundtrack has unity. Soundtracks that have a bit of this and a bit of that, with different orchestrations for each cue and different thematic, rhythmic, and harmonic elements, are not much better than library music.

Composers should think carefully about the following before they start creating music cues:

- Create a unique orchestra of track instruments for each project. It may include synths, samples, acoustic instruments, or a combination of these. Then, compose the entire score, drawing each cue's instruments from your larger project orchestra. Each cue can have a different instrumentation, but taken together, the cues should have instrumental unity.

- Use only a few themes. Create music cues from these themes or parts of them. Remember that themes can be predominantly melodic, but also can be rhythmic, harmonic, or ambient. Sometimes, you can compose a single theme that has several elements such as motifs, rhythms, and harmonies. Each of these can be used for different cues in the project, and all the elements can be brought together for the complete theme in the closing credits.

## WHAT'S NEXT?

Writing music is only part of an interactive composer's job. The other parts—working in a team and taking care of business—are just as important. The final two chapters contain tips on how to share creative responsibilities, market yourself, and operate in a professional working environment.

CHAPTER **11**

# WORKING ENVIRONMENT

Traditional media composers are used to controlling their own musical creations. They're trained to work that way, and expect to be rewarded For producing work that's unique. However, when composers work on interactive media projects in a team setting, they need to learn how to share creative control with the other team members.

## SHARING CREATIVE SPACE

Composers, whether they come from songwriting or orchestral backgrounds, generally create their music alone, using a recording device, computer, or pencil and paper. Their creative space belongs only to themselves. They have been nurtured in a culture that rewards their uniqueness and individuality.

There's a big difference in the training and work environment between creators in the solitary arts, such as music composers, and those who work in the collaborative arts, such as filmmakers and interactive media composers.

From the onset of an interactive (also known as new media) project, a creative team is formed under the direction of a team leader—usually the project producer or production manager. The composer is part of this team from the beginning, as opposed to being brought in after the production is completed, as is common in film and television production. Consequently, composers must share their creative space with others, so it's very important that they are comfortable working in and interacting with a group: being team players.

It turns out that some of the items in your kindergarten report card, principally "Works and Plays Well with Others," are very important when you're part of a new media team. Composers must be prepared and comfortable sharing their creative and musical spaces, while collaborating on a project.

In the early days of new media production, music composers were usually computer coders as well. This was because they had to use specialized authoring tools that were more like computer languages than music sequencers. This ensured that composers felt that they were part of the team.

Today, composers need not be coders, but the same community environment persists, involving composers in the overall creative process, rather than the isolated job of scoring after the rest of the project is completed.

The creative team may be small or large: perhaps only two or three people for a small presentation, or hundreds of creators for a large project. Generally, the team contains about a half dozen key creative people:

- team leader (producer or production supervisor)
- writer

- graphic designer

- interactive designer/technical producer

- coder

- animator and/or videographer/filmmaker

- sound and music designer(s)

If the project is a game, the team will likely be much larger, possibly with section heads for different portions of the game.

The music composer might report to the sound/music designer or might be a member of the creative team directly. In smaller productions, the composer could be responsible for the sound effects, as well.

Being part of a team from the outset of production benefits a composer in many ways. An important psychological benefit is that new media producers rarely throw out complete interactive music scores. Unlike films, where one in five music scores is rejected and the composer is fired in favor of a new one, new media composers don't work with the sword of Damocles dangling over their heads.

The reason is simple. As part of the team, composers start composing demos of music cues as the interactive project is being designed, so everyone has a chance to offer feedback on musical ideas while they are still in progress. In addition, the composer gets to hear early versions of the sound effects. This provides important information about the sonic landscape and helps the composer find synergies between the music and effects. Finally, the music tracks can inspire other members of the team to use their creativity in sync with the music they're hearing.

The time allotted for composition is also very different in interactive media. A game composer may work on a project over a period of eighteen months or more, compared to the average film score that must be completed, start to finish, in about six weeks or less.

## LEAD, FOLLOW, AND COLLABORATE

The key to working in a team is flexibility. A composer isn't hired just to be a passive worker who follows directions, but to contribute and lead creative discussions when appropriate. That means the composer must be familiar with what the other team members do, how their work impacts the music and, most important, how their work affects end users. If you're going to write music for Web sites, you'd better be able to analyze what makes a Web site successful. The same holds true for cellphones, gaming consoles, and presentations.

But being prepared to participate strongly is only one side of the coin. The other side is being able to follow the lead of others. A good team member should be able to move back and forth between the roles of chief and follower, and also be able to collaborate as a peer.

Remember, one of the greatest contributors to the success of a traditional or new media project is focus. The goal is to make each user feel that the property has been developed by a single person with a single vision.

## BE A GOOD LISTENER AND INTERPRETER

No collaboration is possible unless a composer is a good communicator. The problem is, communication is notoriously difficult when it comes to music. There's a saying that music is a universal language, but no one knows how to translate it into a spoken language. Non-musicians are usually at a loss when trying to communicate their musical ideas to composers, and vice versa.

Television and film composer Donald Quan tells of his experience with a producer who hired him because he loved a video demo that Donald sent him. The producer asked Donald to compose the theme music to sound as close as possible to the beat of the demo. Donald followed the producer's wishes, or so he thought, and on the day of the recording was confident that the producer would be pleased with the theme.

On the contrary, the producer came up to him and, with a look of concern on his face, said, "I thought you were going to use the same beat as you did in the demo!" Donald countered with, "But the beat is exactly the same as the demo. I made sure of that, because we spoke about it. The tempo and rhythm are identical."

They were at a standoff until Donald suggested they listen to the demo together. They called for a break in the recording session and, while the cost-clock kept ticking, the engineer played the original demo. The producer's face lit up about twenty seconds into the demo, when he heard a cymbal crash that coincided with an onscreen credit. "There!" he said, triumphantly. "That's the beat you left out!"

The producer was using the word "beat" to describe what composers usually refer to as a "hit." Donald quickly added a cymbal crash to his orchestration at the point that the producer's credit came onscreen, and the session was saved.

One of the most difficult aspects of communication is finding a common language to discuss music with non-musicians. Two tips will help you communicate more effectively:

- Learn to be a good listener. Pay attention to what someone says, and *also* interpret their body language and the way they emphasize certain words and phrases. The meaning is not always in the words that a person speaks, but in *how* they say them.

- Steer clear of musical terms. Producers are sometimes too keen to use these, particularly if they have some knowledge of music, but music terminology can easily be misinterpreted. Instead, discuss the cues in emotional terms, commonly understood metaphors, and concrete examples of projects that you and the producer are both familiar with, to cement the meaning of your musical conversations.

## ACCEPT AND INCORPORATE CRITICISM

Probably the most difficult aspect of communicating with team members and producers is accepting and incorporating their criticism. Much as we try to have thick skins, composers all suffer to some extent from not being able to disassociate criticism of our work from criticism of ourselves.

This is not unreasonable given that music, as an art form, is one of the deepest expressions of our inner selves. When you get criticism that you believe is unwarranted, take a deep breath, relax, and try to evaluate the merits of the criticism from the perspective of the critic.

Sometimes it's worthwhile arguing for your musical ideas, and sometimes a music cue that's had a poor reception at first can grow on others, particularly if it was not what they expected. But . . . pick your battles carefully.

Composers usually write between three and six different themes until they hit on the theme that producers approve. I remember meeting Academy Award–winning composer Maurice Jarre at a recording session and chatting with him about his experience in coming up with the main music theme for *Dr. Zhivago*. He told me he was getting frustrated, because he kept composing themes and presenting them to the producers with no success.

One day, after presenting yet another theme without success, he absentmindedly started noodling a simple phrase on the piano. He turned to the producer, who was now smiling. "That's it!" the producer said. The music, known as "Lara's Theme" (or "Somewhere My Love"), went on to become a huge hit and won him an Oscar.

Even though Jarre's other themes may have been good, the process of accepting the producer's judgment and rewriting the theme many times ultimately produced the right result.

Being a media composer is, in the end, a job. The score to an interactive media production isn't and shouldn't be judged on the merits of the music score as isolated from the project. The ultimate compliment is to have a hit presentation, Web site, or video-game that achieves the objectives of its producers.

## CAUTIONARY WORDS ABOUT SLEEP

If a good night's sleep is necessary for you to do a good job, composing for interactive media—particularly for games—might not be the right profession for you. In these fields, it is common for music to be required in a timeframe that precludes getting a full night's sleep, sometimes for days, weeks, or months on end. But if the idea of a creative collaboration inspires you, then you might find the rewards to be worth the sleepless nights.

## WHAT'S NEXT?

My friend Randy Bachman, of Bachman-Turner Overdrive and the Guess Who, was inspired to write the hit tune "Taking Care of Business" by the lessons he learned in the music business. In short, if you don't take care of your own business, no one else will. The next chapter explains demos, how to market your work, contracts, and the flow of income that can sustain a professional composer.

CHAPTER

# 12

CHAPTER

# FINDING WORK

What's the point of knowing how to ply your craft as an interactive music composer if you don't have an opportunity to work in the field? After you've honed your skills, it's time to market yourself, find work, and maximize your financial returns.

# YOUR DEMO DISK

A *demo disk* is your most valuable tool for getting work. It's a portfolio of your music, demonstrating to prospective employers that you have composing skills. If you're talented and lucky, a prospective employer will find your demo music engaging and attractive, and may even find it suitable for use in a project.

You already have the makings of a demo disk if you've completed the exercises in this book. Your **DemoMusic** folder contains many music cues that you can include on your demo. These should be arranged in folders as follows:

- **Advertisements**
  WebAd.wav

- **Earcons**
  AddressEarcon.wav
  ApplicationsEarcon.wav
  CalendarEarcon.wav
  NotesEarcon.wav
  SyncEarcon.wav

- **Functions**
  Action1.wav
  Action2.wav
  Arabian.wav
  Character.wav
  Dramatic1.wav
  Dramatic2.wav
  Humor1.wav
  Humor2.wav
  Pastoral.wav
  Race.wav
  Urban.wav

- **Games**
  Game.wav
  GameAttractor.wav
  GameCredits.wav
  GameEndingSuccess.wav
  GameFailure.wav
  GameSituation1.wav
  GameSituation2.wav
  GameSituation3.wav
  GameStartup.wav
  GameSuccess.wav

RPG.wav
RPGAttractor.wav
RPGCredits.wav
RPGFailure.wav
RPGSituation1.wav
RPGSituation2.wav
RPGSituation3.wav
RPGStartup.wav
RPGSuccess.wav
RPGUltimateFailure.wav
RPGUltimateSuccess.wav
Strategy.wav
StrategyAttractor.wav
StrategyCredits.wav
StrategyFailure.wav
StrategySituation1.wav
StrategySituation2.wav
StrategySituation3.wav
StrategyStartup.wav
StrategySuccess.wav
StrategyUltimateFailure.wav
StrategyUltimateSuccess.wav
Twitch.wav
TwitchAttractor.wav
TwitchCredits.wav
TwitchFailure.wav
TwitchSituation1.wav
TwitchSituation2.wav
TwitchSituation3.wav
TwitchStartup.wav
TwitchSuccess.wav
TwitchUltimateFailure.wav
TwitchUltimateSuccess.wav

- **Logos**
  LogoAppliance.wav

- **Loops**
  DrumGroove01.wav
  LoopMix.wav

- **Songs**
  NarrativeSong.wav

- **Themes**
  BadMonster.wav
  Heroine.wav
  TVloop.wav
  TVsad.wav
  TVtheme.wav
  TVupbeat.wav

- **Web Pages**
  GouldHomePage.wav
  InfoWebPage.wav
  PageMusicHTML.wav
  PromoWebPage.wav
  ShoppingWebPage.wav

You can change the folder structure to suit your preference, and add subfolders and new folders as appropriate.

Burn (copy to a CD or DVD) these music cues, along with any others that you've composed for interactive media. This will be your *Music Library* disk. Eventually, you will have many *Library* disks, each filled with music cues that you've composed.

Don't make the mistake of including all your work on your demos. Your complete *Library* includes everything: your best work, your average work, and your work that's below par. It also has too many cues for most prospective employers to listen to. (They rarely listen to more than a dozen.) Finally, some of your cues will likely sound similar, so you will want to choose only the best example of that type of work and leave the others off your demo.

Cues on your *Demo Disk* should be chosen to demonstrate your:

- versatility

- musical proficiency

- production proficiency

- familiarity with interactive media projects

Depending on which market you're targeting for work, your demo may contain music cues that demonstrate your facility with:

- identity, theme, leitmotif

- drama

- action

- humor

- songwriting

- setting

- atmosphere

It's a good idea to burn a custom demo disk for each job interview you can get, based on what you can learn about each company you pitch for work. These custom demos are different from your general demo disk, which you might send to all potential clients.

## MARKETING YOURSELF AND YOUR WORK

The starting point for any marketing campaign, including marketing yourself for work, is to qualify potential clients. There are two main approaches. If you have your mind set on doing a particular type of project, such as corporate presentations, you should focus all your energy on potential clients that produce presentations and exhaustively contact each of them for appointments.

In this case, you would tailor your demo disk to focus on music cues appropriate to presentations. You would include cues that illustrate corporate and information IDs and atmospheric loops that work well under a presenter's spoken words, generally avoiding dramatic ups and downs except for cues intended to build to the closing theme.

For Web work, you would focus your demo music on short musical IDs and a selection of animation, game, and advertising loops. You might add a few short dramatic cues to illustrate your ability to score mini-dramas.

For videogame work, you can include longer cues that illustrate your knowledge of twitch, RPG, strategy, simulation, and instructional games. For one or two of these, you could include short examples of a complete package, including attractor, startup, situation, success, failure, and closing credit cues.

For mobile media work, the general rule would be: keep it short. Since the number of categories for mobile projects is growing, you could include a variety of music cue types, as enumerated above, but with an emphasis on short lengths. You might also produce these at high compression ratios (small sizes) and indicate on your demo disk that the production quality has been optimized for quick download to mobile platforms.

If you're not sure which type of projects you want to focus on, or if you'd prefer to do a mix of different types of projects, you should use a more general marketing strategy, targeting potential clients in all areas of interactive projects with a general demo disk that has a taste of this and that. In this case, your general demo disk package should invite the potential client to request one of your themed demo disks: presentations, Web, videogame, and mobile media. If you get a nibble from a producer, you can then produce a demo disk that's targeted to the client's business, and you have a leg up because you can get back to the client and ask some questions that will help you target your demo music material.

# FINDING WORK

Interactive media companies and companies with new media departments are always looking for good composers who understand their projects and who know the tools and lingo of the trade. The first hurdle you have to overcome, therefore, is finding the names and contact information for these companies—ones that are located within your geographic area. You may wish to restrict your work area to the town or city where you live, or you may be willing to relocate to another place if you get a job. Interactive media companies and companies with new media departments are located much more widely than companies that produce movies and television programs. You may be surprised to find some companies producing the kinds of projects you'd like to work on in your hometown.

You might find your potential employers by using Internet search engines to find national and local trade associations of interactive media companies. Since companies that do interactive projects use different terms to define their work, you should search for new media associations, interactive media associations, and digital media associations. The home pages of these sites usually have lists of member companies. Add them to your list of potential employers.

For interactive production departments in large companies, you need to take a different approach and do more research. Start by calling your local chamber of commerce. Tell them that you're looking for employment with a company that has an in-house audio/visual department. They may be able to help you with some company names. If they can't, ask them for a list of the largest companies in your work area. Then, make cold calls to these companies, asking to speak with someone in the audio/visual or new media department. You'll likely strike out with some companies, and find that some companies have a/v departments in different locations, but hopefully you will hit pay dirt with a few companies in your area. Bear in mind that the harder it is to find a potential employer, the harder it is for other composers to locate that company, so there should be less competition for the available work.

Once you have your list of targeted companies, start contacting them by phone and e-mail. It's helpful to do some detective work about a company before your contact with them. You can use the

Web to find basic information about potential clients, and you can chat with receptionists and other employees on the phone and even when you're waiting for your interview, to get a sense of the organization's current projects and priorities.

Tell your potential clients that you're a composer, looking for work composing soundtracks for their PowerPoint, Web, game, or mobile media projects. Let them know that you are a keen and enthusiastic person, prepared to work long hours when a project is on a short deadline. You'll likely find that, even if a company that you contact is not currently in the market for your music services today, they may recommend you to another company that is, or they may keep your name on file until they need you.

Composers, like anyone else looking for work, should present themselves well, both in person and in their résumés. You should be enthusiastic about the prospect of working with the organization and on the organization's projects, and you should express your comfort with working in a team environment.

## BUSINESS ARRANGEMENTS

Most interactive music composition agreements have been buyouts. In a buyout, the composer is paid a fixed sum of money and gets no residuals or royalties, no matter how successful the property may be. You get payment and your employer gets the ownership of the music that you compose.

Industrial practice has been different in the television and film industries. In those media, composers are entitled to various "back-end" royalty payments, primarily for what's known as "performance rights." Performance rights, which include the right to communicate music to the public, are paid to music composers and publishers when radio stations, television stations, Web sites, and myriad other users, including restaurants and bars, play music. They pay performing rights collectives (PROs) royalties, and the collectives pass appropriate portions of their collections to composers for the use of their musical works.

In addition, television and film composer agreements frequently have provisions for other kinds of royalties, such as mechanical and reproduction royalties, which are paid when copies are made of music in DVDs, CDs, sheet music, and the like. An excellent resource that explains the complicated world of royalties and fees for media composers is *And Now... The Soundtrack Business.* This DVD is available from the Guild of Canadian Film Composers at www.gcfc.ca. Excellent books on this subject are *Making Music Make Money* by Eric Beall (Berklee Press, 2004) and *Music Publishing 101* by George Howard (Berklee Press 2004).

The practice of buying out all the music rights for interactive media is beginning to change as many interactive media works move to the Web and to mobile phones. PROs, such as BMI and ASCAP, have started collecting royalties when music is distributed on the Web. They generally pay composers half the royalties collected. The publisher gets the other half. The Society of Composers and Lyricists (SCL) in Hollywood and the Guild of Canadian Film Composers (GCFC) in Canada are two composer organizations that you can contact for more information about interactive media rights and contracts.

# TECHNICAL INFO

There are many production and technical issues that affect the way a score is composed. Here are some key insights into them.

# DOWNLOADING AND STREAMING MUSIC

Downloading sends a file across the Internet and makes a copy onto a user's hard drive or other storage device. It can take a short or long time depending on how powerful the server and device are, and how fast the Internet infrastructure is between them.

The download time also depends on how large a file is. While it's obvious that music file size depends on how long the music is, it's not always apparent how the music compression technology affects the file size. Uncompressed full-fidelity music files, like the ones in music CDs, are about 10 megabytes (MB) for each minute of stereo music. That's usually expressed as 10 MB/min. A 60-minute album requires about 600 MB of storage—almost all of a CD's capacity.

Compression technologies make it possible to make music files smaller without changing their duration. Codecs compress the music files for storage and transmission, then expand (decompress) them for playback.

**MP3** is one of many music file **codecs**. An MP3 music file can be highly compressed, perhaps to one hundredth its original size. That reduces the transmission requirements to 1/10 MB/min, but the fidelity loss is significant. On the other hand, an MP3 file may be gently compressed, perhaps to one tenth its original size, requiring a transfer rate of 1 MB/minute. In this case, the quality remains quite acceptable, about the same as FM radio.

When you log onto music Web sites to download music files for temping or for inclusion in your final mixes, you'll often see quality indicators listed as a rate of playback—64 kbs (kilobits per second), for example. You can convert that indicator into megabytes/minute by the following formula:

**MB/min** = (kbs × 60 ) / (1000 × 8) = **kbs × 0.0075**

So, 64 kbs = 0.48 MB/min—better than the very low quality of 0.1 MB/min, but not as good as FM quality of 1 MB/min. MP3 files at 128 kbs are considered similar in quality to FM radio. Using the formula, 128 kbs = 0.96 MB/min—about 1 MB/min.

**Streaming** is another type of online music delivery. When music is **streamed**, it must be capable of traveling from the server disk, through the Internet, and to your computer at least as fast as the music file is played on your computer. A streamed file, strictly speaking, need not be copied onto your hard disk. It can play as an ephemeral (temporary) experience, entering your computer's random access memory (RAM), playing through speakers or headphones, and then being erased as the next chunk of music is played.

Since a file traveling through the Internet is subject to random delays due to Internet traffic, the Internet connection needs to be faster than the streamed file speed. Otherwise, the slightest delay in file transfer would cause your music to sputter and stop. Since 128 kbps is considered a reasonable quality for music, the user's Internet connection needs to be faster than that, which means that dial-up modems, which max out at 64 kbs, won't work for decent-quality streamed audio. If video is sent along with music, the connection needs to be faster yet.

In order to have music properly synchronized with Web pages at reasonable quality, users need to have high-speed connections. High-speed (sometimes called "broadband") connections usually use a cable television line or phone line, along with a cable modem or DSL (Direct Subscriber Line) modem. Wireless high-speed Internet alternatives are rapidly gaining ground, however, particularly the IEEE 802.11 standard, commonly known as Wi-Fi. Many industry analysts believe wireless will ultimately overtake wired Internet connections because they will be cheaper to install and have higher speed potentials.

## AUDIO FILE FORMATS

There are many different file formats available for music and general audio. You should be familiar with all of them because you will likely need to convert from one format to another in order to gain compatibility with your software applications.

The following formats are *lossless*. They take up the most space but do not degrade the sound quality.

> **AIFF**—Audio Interchange File Format—is uncompressed 8-, 16-, 24-, or 32-bit audio, and can be mono or stereo. The file extension is usually ".aif."

**WAV** files are similar to aiff, and are recognized as native by the Windows OS. The extension is ".wav."

**Sound Designer** types **I** and **II** are similar to WAV and AIFF, but they contain additional information about audio regions and markers. They are native to Digidesign's Pro Tools applications. The file extensions are ".sd1" and ".sd2."

The following audio formats use variable compression rates, all of which are *lossy*, and create files that are much smaller. Most can be used at different compression ratios, to make files smaller with less fidelity, or larger with greater fidelity. Once an audio file is compressed with a lossy codec, you can never recover the full fidelity of the original file.

**MP3** is the most popular online compression format. Its full name is "MPEG1 audio layer 3." **MPEG** stands for Moving Picture Experts Group, an international body that defines standards for digital video and audio files. The file extension is ".mp3."

**AAC**—Advanced Audio Coding—is a newer and improved format that was designed for MPEG 4, the successor to MPEG 1, 2, and 3. It can accommodate up to 48 channels of audio at up to 96 kHz sample rates. The file extension is ".mp4."

**QuickTime Audio** is a cross-platform and multi-operating-system format from Apple. It can accommodate many different audio formats within its structure, including MP3, MP4, AIFF, WAV, and MIDI. The file extension is ".mov."

**Shockwave Audio** is Macromedia's file format used for Flash and Shockwave players. Similar to QuickTime Audio, it can accommodate many different audio formats within its structure. The file extension is ".swa."

**Real Media Audio** is Real Network's proprietary audio format. The file extension is ".rma."

**Audio on Unix** (AU) is used with the Unix OS and Linux OS, as well as with the Java programming language. The file extension is ".au."

**Musical Instrument Digital Interface** (**MIDI**) is used when synthesizers are available at the user end and very high compression is needed. The extension is ".mid."

The formats used by mobile phones are special cases, frequently proprietary, and covered in chapter 9. As mobile media acquire larger memories and greater connection bandwidth, it's expected that they will start using the more common formats described above. This has already occurred in the videogame industry, which originally used highly compressed and proprietary formats, but is now using more common formats such as MP3 and WAV.

# SAMPLE RATE

The sample rate is the *frequency* of samples (number per second) taken from a continuous signal, such as a sound captured by a microphone, as it's transformed into a discrete digital signal, made up of a series of ones and zeros. For example, the digital files on music CDs all have a sample rate of 44,100 per second. That means there are forty-four thousand one hundred numbers stored in the file for each second of each channel of music. No wonder digital audio files require so much storage and bandwidth.

The highest frequency you can reproduce from a digital file is half the sample frequency. Consequently, if you want to be able to reproduce a 20 kHz sound frequency, generally taken to be the upper limit of most people's hearing, you need to sample at least forty thousand times a second.

# BIT DEPTH

The *bit depth* of a signal describes the number of bits used to specify the level (loudness) of a digital audio sample. In the binary language of digital numbers, eight bits can represent up to 256 different levels, sixteen bits can represent up to 65,536 levels, twenty-four bits can represent 16,777,216 levels, and so on. As the sound plays back from sample to sample at the sample rate (see above), finer gradations between samples result in smoother sounds. So, more bits result in a more accurate reproduction of the original sound.

Bit depth has a direct correlation to the dynamic range of a sound—the number of gradations from soft to loud. Files on a normal music CD have a bit depth of sixteen bits, which translates into 96 dB of dynamic range. Since symphony orchestras can have a dynamic range in live performance of greater than 100 dB, this standard is excellent, but not perfect. Newer audio standards frequently use twenty-four or more bits for super fidelity. Of course, the greater the bit depth, the larger the file.

## WET OR DRY?

You can move musical parts forward or backward in the final mix using reverb instead of level. The *wetter* (more reverb) a part has, the further back and less intrusive it becomes in the mix. The *drier* (less reverb) it is, the more it moves forward and sticks out.

## SURROUND SOUND

The music production standards for interactive media have been getting higher, including the number and types of tracks that must be delivered. Console games, for example, compete for consumer dollars with movies. And movies are mixed in multi-channel surround-sound formats such as Dolby 5.1 or THX surround (left, right, center, left-rear, right-rear, and a subwoofer channel). Now that games are approaching films in the quality of their images and are being played on home-theater systems with surround-sound audio, game producers are starting to request music and sound effects to be delivered in these formats.

This gives composers new creative options such as placing soft ambient pads in the rear and instruments up front with their reverbs behind. It also adds significant complexity to the mixing sessions. For surround sound, a composer needs:

- a professional quality sequencer and mixer.

- an audio monitoring system (preamp + amps + speakers) that are properly calibrated for surround sound.

- an acoustically balanced room so the surround effects can be properly auditioned. Unfortunately, you can no longer use a good set of headphones to audition your mixes, when mixing surround. They don't work with multichannel surround sound.

- knowledge about surround sound in general and information about the industrial practices of your client's technical crew.

# DELIVERY AND BACKUP MEDIA

It wasn't so long ago that analog cassettes were the major distribution media for audio and video. The enormous advantage of digital media, in which every copy has exactly the same fidelity as the original content, has resulted in a replacement of these media with CDs, DVDs, and MiniDV-format videotapes. In addition to these consumer media, professionals in the a/v field use digital cassette tapes in DA-88 (Hi8), ADAT (VHS), DVCPro (MiniDV), DV50 (MiniDV), and Beta SP formats, as well as reel-to-reel 1-inch and 2-inch digital tapes.

Although post-production team members may use one or more of these media types, composers generally use CDs and DVDs to exchange audio and video information. The more sophisticated your production operation is, the more likely you are to have the other formats, particularly DA-88s for multitrack audio.

The question of backup media is not trivial. Every time you start a new project, you'll have to wipe your music files from your hard disks in order to make room for the new ones. And you'll have to save all of these files, in case you need to reconstruct the mixes or do different mixes at a later date. Be prepared to spend significant time, energy, and money to set up and maintain a backup system that not only stores your work but also makes it easy for you to locate a particular file at a later date. There are many disk cataloging programs—some of them freeware and shareware—that do an excellent job of maintaining a catalog of your files, even as they are distributed over many backup disks or tapes.

# WRAP-UP

The material in this book covers a broad range of information. Some is technical, such as how to use loops and sequencers; some is general, about interactive media; some deals with the psychological impacts of marrying music with visual images; some is specific to a media type, such as videogames; and some will help you get a job as a professional composer.

The exercises were designed to hone your skills as a composer, giving you opportunities and challenges to compose music for a wide variety of interactive project scenarios. If you've done all the exercises, you should be on your way to proficiency as a composer for presentations, Web, games, and mobile media. You will also be well on your way to having a good demo disk, which you can use to procure work.

The understanding and skills you've acquired in this book will be helpful to you whether music composition is your hobby or profession. The practice you've gained in analyzing music and how it relates to its compositional formats will assist you whether you decide to specialize in composing for interactive media, linear media, or just music for its own sake.

Best of luck.

Keep the flame burning.

*Paul Hoffert*

# ABOUT THE AUTHOR

**Paul Hoffert** is Chair of the Guild of Canadian Film Composers and former Chair of the Academy of Canadian Cinema and Television. He is a Faculty Fellow at Harvard University and a Fine Arts Professor at York University.

At 16, he was performing on network television and recorded his first album. By the time he was 22, he had composed several feature film scores and written an Off-Broadway musical. In 1969, he founded Lighthouse, a rock group that earned nine Gold, Platinum, and Diamond Record Awards for hits such as "One Fine Morning," "Sunny Days," and "Pretty Lady."

He is a best-selling author of books that detail how to thrive in the information age. He is a pioneer of creating and understanding interactive content, and in 2001 received the Pixel Award as the new media industry's Visionary. In 2005, he received the Order of Canada, that country's highest honor, for his contributions to music and media.

# INDEX

**Note:** Page numbers in *italics* indicate figures.

# Want More?

Berkleemusic is the online extension school of Berklee College of Music. Study music production online from anywhere in the world with Berklee's world-renowned faculty.

Produce great-sounding music at home using the software and sequencers in **Reason, Ableton Live, Digital Performer, Logic, Sonar,** and **Pro Tools**.

**Online Courses and Certificate Programs Enrolling Now**
- Mixing and Mastering with Pro Tools 12-week course
- Critical Listening 12-week course
- Master Certificate in Production 8-course program
- Specialist Certificate in Electronic Music Production 3-course program

Call Our Student Advisors Today
**1.866.BERKLEE**
www.berkleemusic.com

Berklee music™
learn music online